(Amused   June 3)

DAILY LIFE IN ENGLAND IN THE REIGN OF GEORGE III

Daily Life SERIES

Temple Bar at the beginning of the reign of George III

ANDRÉ PARREAUX

DAILY LIFE IN ENGLAND IN THE REIGN OF GEORGE III

Translated by Carola Congreve

London
GEORGE ALLEN AND UNWIN LTD

SBN 04 942077 1

Translated from the French
LA VIE QUOTIDIENNE EN ANGLETERRE AU TEMPS
DE GEORGE III
© Hachette, 1966

PRINTED IN GREAT BRITAIN
in 10 on 12 point Baskerville type by
BUTLER AND TANNER LTD
FROME AND LONDON

FOREWORD

The record that follows covers the period between the accession of George III in 1760 and the Regency Act of 1810—after this date the King's insanity remained incurable, with intermittent periods of lucidity. From 1811 until the death of George III in 1820 England was ruled by the Prince of Wales as Regent.

CONTENTS

ILLUSTRATIONS

INTRODUCTION

THE REIGN OF GEORGE III

Queen Anne, the daughter of James II and last sovereign of Stuart blood, died in 1714. After her death the throne of England was occupied by a series of German princes who thus became Kings of England as well as Electors of Hanover; George I (1714–27), George II (1727–60), and finally George III. The first two Georges remained fundamentally attached to their Teutonic electorate, but George III, brought up in England by English tutors, was obliged to take a much greater interest in English affairs than had his grandfather (George II), or his great-grandfather. Both his predecessors had on two occasions good reason to fear expulsion from England by a Stuart pretender; but when the risings of 1715 and 1745 failed, the Hanoverian dynasty became secure at last against the threat of the Jacobites. Accordingly, the reign of George III, who succeeded to the throne in 1760, was overshadowed not by dynastic issues but by problems of government and of national expansion.

END OF THE SEVEN YEARS WAR

By 1760 the Seven Years War between France, Austria and Russia on the one hand, and England and Prussia on the other, had lasted for four years. Encouraged by William Pitt the Elder, England had conducted a determined and successful campaign against French positions in Canada, Africa, the West Indies and India, while Frederick II of Prussia, through his own military genius and the financial assistance afforded him by the English, succeeded, with alternate bouts of victory and defeat, in restraining the French and Austrian military power on the continent of Europe. But when in 1761 the Earl of Bute, a Scottish nobleman and personal friend and adviser to the King, became Secretary of State, his efforts within the cabinet in favour of peace forced Pitt's resignation. Although in 1762 Spain had entered the war upon the side of the French, new successes in the West Indies, as well as difficulties in Europe with Frederick the Great, had reinforced the position of the peace party. In 1763 the Treaty of Paris assigned Canada to England, together with the whole of that part of Louisiana which lies to the east of Mississippi, as well as Cape Breton and the Saint Lawrence Islands. England also retained Tobago, San Domingo, St Vincent and others, but restored to France the islands of Guadeloupe, Martinique, Désirade and St Lucia. Of her African possessions France retained Senegal, but relinquished Gorée, while the trading posts in India were restored to France on condition that she did not in future fortify them, and that, further, she would acknowledge the supremacy of the East India Company.

THE AMERICAN REVOLUTION

The Seven Years War had been a costly affair, and, in order to solve the financial difficulties arising from it, it was necessary to impose new taxes (upon consumer goods) and to increase excise duties. What is more, the Government in London, insisting that the war had benefited the American colonists, decided to make them contribute towards the expenses of keeping up the British Army and Navy, in their turn specifically responsible for suppression of the smuggling which was unscrupulously resorted to by the colonists to supply their own needs. The colonists themselves were of the opinion that they had already paid in large part for the campaigns against Canada. Further, the attempt in 1765 to impose upon them a so-called stamp duty, levied on all official documents, invited protest in the name of the principle of 'no taxation without representation'. Stamp duty in America was an innovation which, according to the American assemblies, the American legislature alone had the right to impose. In the face of these protests, the English Parliament decided a year later to annul the stamp duty, but the central government and the colonists were each equally determined to shift on to the other the financial burden of defence for the American colonies. In 1767 the imposition of customs duties upon certain products (especially tea) at point of entry into America met with determined opposition from the colonists, many of whom pledged themselves never to buy these products. In some colonies imports from the mother country declined by 50 per cent, and in 1770 England was forced to waive all customs duties except those attached to the import of tea. The great majority of colonists refused to buy tea which had been so imported, while smuggled tea, lower in price, attracted a large number of customers. To put an end to this state of affairs the British Government in 1773 authorized the East India Company to import tea into America direct, free of duty: a measure which succeeded in reducing by one half the price of tea in America, thus discouraging smuggling. But on December 16 of that year the citizens of Boston emptied into the sea the cargoes of three tea clippers belonging to the Company. The British Government retaliated by closing Boston harbour and modifying the constitution of Massachusetts to authorize the Crown to nominate Councillors, hitherto elected by the House of Representatives. These measures succeeded in encouraging the colonists to unite more resolutely against the mother country. In 1775 the Lexington skirmish heralded a war which was to last eight years.

In the Declaration of Independence signed in 1776 the colonies disclaimed all allegiance to the Crown and declared their political separation from Great Britain.

The initial successes of the British forces—largely consisting of mercenaries provided by German princes who were well pleased to augment their incomes, and of native tribesmen—were followed by the first important American victory in October 1777, which compelled the capitulation at Saratoga of the British General Burgoyne. It was this victory which persuaded first France, then Spain, to support the American colonies with arms—while, in 1780, Russia, Sweden, Denmark and Holland drafted a treaty of armed neutrality *vis-à-vis* Britain, in this way uniting those countries which normally provided the timber and the hemp required by the British Navy. For the first time for many years the Fleet no longer dominated the seas: the surrender in 1781 of the British General Cornwallis at Yorktown was in part the consequence of the blockade of the American coast by the French Admiral de Grasse. Rodney's victory in the Saints failed to re-establish British supremacy, and in 1782 England was forced to recognize the independence of the United States.

Meanwhile the American revolution had been having its effects upon the domestic policy of England.

ENGLAND AWAKES TO MODERN POLITICAL LIFE

During the peace negotiations with France in 1762 one of the most active opponents of the Government had been John Wilkes, whose journal *The North Briton* attacked the Court with a vehemence which appealed especially to the middle-class Londoner. The aristocratic leaders of the opposition, however, regarded Wilkes as a dangerous ally, because of his disquieting tendency to seek support from the lower classes in London. Arrested under an illegal warrant, Wilkes instituted proceedings against certain of those responsible and eventually obtained damages. But in 1763 the Government, thanks to somewhat questionable procedures, succeeded in expelling Wilkes from the Commons and a year later he was declared an outlaw. Wilkes retired to voluntary exile on the Continent, from whence he returned to England and stood as parliamentary candidate for the county of Middlesex. He was elected, arrested again, fined and sentenced to ten months in prison—after which, in 1769, he was once more expelled from Parliament. On the fourth occasion he was again returned, but since on this occasion he was opposed the House of Commons declared him incapable of sitting and his opponent was duly elected. It was precisely this manifestation of political flexibility which so commanded the admiration of the French *philosophes* of the day, not, at least on the face of it, without reason—since, as one modern historian has pointed out, there is nothing to be gained by bribery if force alone is enough.

Wilkes was bound to be admitted to Parliament after the General Election of 1774, but his parliamentary activities were in no way remarkable. It was in the political battles which raged outside Parliament that he had played his most important part. In the course of these he had by force of circumstances become the hero of the masses and of the common people of London; for ten years the cry 'for Wilkes and Liberty' rang out at every street demonstration. When the American War of Independence broke out Wilkes became the spokesman of the rebel English colonists, and so he continued, even when the American cause began to lose its popular appeal. But Wilkes' reputation in history is explained by the interest that was fostered in his own case to an extent where public opinion was alerted and organized. The Society for the

14

Defence of the Declaration of Rights, founded in 1769 (with, in Wilkes' view, the paying of his own debts as its principal aim), was sustained by London tradesmen at odds with the economic policy of the Government. After the 1780 riots, 'anti-Papist' in name, but in fact a reflection of social unrest among the working classes, Wilkes ceased to exert much further influence; as London magistrate he was responsible for calling out the military to suppress the rioters. Between 1767 and 1772 the anonymous *Letters of Junius*, although they were not the work of Wilkes, also helped to discredit the Government.

Wilkes' agitation, Junius' pamphlets, the successes of the American colonists, were so many blows aimed at the oligarchic system of parliamentary and electoral corruption upon which English political life in the eighteenth century was founded. Certainly the Society for Constitutional Information founded in 1780 by Major John Cartwright, and stimulated by events in America, was rather too advanced in its views to attract the leaders of the opposition. But the Association founded in 1779 was a different matter. Its appeal varied greatly from region to region, Middlesex being unquestionably the most daring; but it was in Yorkshire, perhaps, where the Association managed to undermine the hegemony of the noble families, that it scored its most lasting success. On a national scale the work of the Association did not amount to much. Its greatest merit lay in the experiments it carried out with methods of organization, which Wilberforce was later to copy in his campaign against the slave trade. But the sectors of society which resisted the 'reformers', together with the 'anti-Papist' violence which arose in London in 1780 in the name of the extreme protestants in England (the Gordon Riots), led by Lord George Gordon, and finally the astute manœuvres on the part of William Pitt the Younger, who was well aware of how to play the part of honest reformer, all helped to discredit these societies and their actions. In fact, the second Pitt was a protégé of the East India Company, which helped him financially in his efforts to oust his rivals, Fox and Shelburne. Corruption was too much an integral part of English politics to be suppressed; eloquent proof of this was provided by the measures used to ensure the victory of Pitt in the General Election of 1784.

The final endeavour of the reformers, before the explosion of the French Revolution, was the centenary celebration in 1788 by the Society for the Commemoration of the Glorious Revolution, of the expulsion of James II. But when in 1792 the Society of Friends of the People endeavoured to rally the leisured classes to some idea of moderate measures of reform, it was too late. The majority of the reformers, not merely those drawn from the aristocracy, but also those from the middle classes themselves, alarmed by the excesses of the French Revolution, were ready to change their allegiance in earnest support of the 'admirable constitution' of Britain.

REACTION IN ENGLAND TO THE FRENCH REVOLUTION

When the French Revolution broke out, the ruling class in England lost no time in discovering the most eloquent interpreter of their hostility and fears in the person of the Irishman Burke, whose *Reflections on the French Revolution*, published in 1790, caused many of the Whigs to rally round Pitt, then leader of the government and of the reorganized Tory party. On the other side, the response of the English-born American Tom Paine, published in London in 1791–92 under the title *The Rights of Man*, reverberated deeply in the hearts of English liberals. Government repression soon made itself felt, while in Birmingham and elsewhere the local magistrates tolerated or even incited violent rioting, aimed at the homes of dissident Protestants and friends of the French Revolution. Only the small group of Whigs around Charles James Fox remained faithful to the ideal of political reform within the existing framework.

More advanced elements in favour of a truly democratic reform founded the Corresponding Society in London, to work for universal suffrage and annual parliaments. This society, made up from members of the artisan and lower middle class of London, did not succeed in winning over completely the industrial region in the North of England. It is true that there was a Society for Political Information in Nottingham, and in Norwich a Constitutional Society, as there also was in Sheffield, but the latter, designed to appeal to the lower classes, alienated the more moderate middle classes. The fears inspired within the leisured section of the population by the propaganda of reformers led to Pitt's suspending Habeas Corpus in 1794—the statute which gave accused people legal rights, and which had attracted the admiration of enlightened

Frenchmen throughout the eighteenth century. The Corresponding Society was declared illegal; Paine's book, *The Rights of Man* was banned, while a system of informers and espionage designed to reveal those suspected of Jacobinism was put into force, at the instigation, and sometimes with the connivance, of the public authorities. Thus in 1792 the magistrate, John Reeves, taking advantage of government support, founded an Association for the Safeguarding of Liberty and Property against Republicans and Levellers, and this fought with any weapons (including anonymous denunciation) all liberal tendencies. A parallel action was pursued by the Society for the Suppression of Vice, which did not limit its action to the moral field, but likewise conducted a vendetta against subversive literature.

In 1793 England began a war against France which, except for a brief interval in 1802, was to linger on until 1814. Her naval supremacy was never challenged, but the expenses of the war, and the subsidies poured out to her continental allies, led to grave financial difficulties, the main burden of which was borne by the workers and the most humble of the urban classes. But while the standard of living amongst the latter continually degenerated, those owning land made profits from the rise in agricultural prices, while the Government's financial policy provided rich opportunities to moneylenders, to those who supplied the Army and Navy, and to financiers and speculators. According to Cobbett, 'There always was among the creatures and close adherents of Mr Pitt a strange mixture of profligacy and cant: jobbers all the morning and Methodists in the afternoon.'

But it was in Ireland perhaps more than in England that the French Revolution showed the most spectacular if not the most sweeping consequences.

THE IRISH QUESTION

The American Revolution had called into being in 1779 a force of Irish volunteer soldiers, designed in theory to protect Ireland against the threat of invasion. In fact, the majority of these volunteers considered themselves as an army of national liberation. But their leaders, drawn from among the aristocracy and upper middle class, having exploited the movement in order to obtain commercial freedom and recognition of independence for their parliament in Dublin (no less oligarchic and corrupt than Parliament in London), disbanded the organization.

In 1791 a young lawyer from Belfast, Wolfe Tone, convinced that the volunteers had been betrayed in 1781, attempted with his society of United Irishmen to create a solid movement towards national independence. Unfortunately the French Directory, instead of offering the Irish the backing they counted upon, missed their chance of invading Ireland when the mutinies of 1797 broke out in the English Navy. The Irish risings of 1798 were not widespread, and when the French disembarked (moreover in insufficient numbers), the rebellion had already been crushed. In 1803 an attempt at rebellion led by Robert Emmet was put down even more abruptly. And yet these risings showed that Ireland was one of the weaker links in the chain of British imperialism; if Bonaparte's efforts had been concentrated upon Ireland instead of dissipated in oriental conquests in the traditional, but never decisive grand manner, the outcome of the struggle between France and England might have been otherwise.

When this duel was over George III had been off the throne for four years; his madness, until now recurring only in phases, with the worst crises arising in 1765, 1788 and 1804, was in 1811 considered to be incurable. When he died in 1820 the Prince of Wales had already been Regent for ten years before succeeding him as George IV. The scene we are about to consider encompasses English life between the accession of George III in 1760 up to the time of his departure from political life in 1810.

PART ONE

COUNTRY LIFE

CHAPTER ONE

THE UPPER CLASSES

HOUSING

An essential and intrinsic feature of the eighteenth-century aristocrat was his possession of a country house. The aristocracy did not simply inhabit these houses; it lived in them in the full sense of the term. The great stately home was very much more than a dwelling: it was the outward sign of the authority and enduring quality of the great families. Material requirements alone do not explain the breadth, magnificence and studied splendour of such palaces as Chatsworth in Derbyshire, of Blenheim near Oxford, Castle Howard and Wentworth Woodhouse in Yorkshire, Seaton Delaval in Northumberland, of Houghton and Holkham Hall in Norfolk, of Woburn Abbey in Bedfordshire and of many more. These princely homes are impressive, undoubtedly so, but they are also a dramatic expression of the remarkable power wielded by the Whig aristocracy, itself supporter and protector of a Hanoverian dynasty which owed to this ruling class its presence on the throne, and which in exchange guaranteed it a privileged position. The country residence emphasized to each great family its own social superiority and political influence. Chatsworth to the Dukes of Devonshire, Blenheim to the Dukes of Marlborough, Castle Howard to the Earls of Carlisle, Seaton Delaval to the Delavals, Holkham Hall to the Earls of Leicester, Houghton to the Earls of Orford, Woburn Abbey to the Dukes of Bedford, and Wentworth Woodhouse to the Marquises of Rockingham and so on. Gazing at these colossal buildings one is aware that their purely functional purpose was of only secondary importance in the eyes of these magnates.

And yet when George III came to the throne the splendid century of the Whig aristocracy was drawing to a close. Not that it was in immediate danger of disappearance—quite the reverse. While its authority in court circles was no longer quite so acceptable, nor yet so freely exerted in central Government, locally its standing was

stronger than ever. Thus, for example, under the first two Georges
Sir Robert Walpole demolished the village of Houghton, which
had grown up around his family mansion, and rebuilt it elsewhere.
In the same way, Viscount Cobham in Buckinghamshire removed
the inhabitants of Stowe to Dadford, on the grounds that they surrounded his mansion too closely. There are many stories of this
kind in the reign of George III; there was, perhaps, a lessening of
influence of Whig authority in the field of national politics, but its
power in its own sphere of provincial life was still autocratic.
When Sir Nathaniel Curzon, the fifth baronet, later the first Lord
Scarsdale, replaced his Queen Anne house with an enormous Palladian building, between the years 1758 to 1768, he decided that
the neighbouring village spoilt his view, and he did not think
twice about transferring it to a more discreet position. In the same
way and at about the same time the first Earl of Harcourt uprooted
the inhabitants of Nuneham Courtenay and erected for them two
rows of fine brick-built houses bordering the Oxford to Henley
road. In 1791, Henry Cornwall Legh, of the opinion that his house
High Lea (near Knutsford in Cheshire) was too close to the main
road, did not re-site his own house, but instead caused the road to
be diverted; and while the work was being carried out gave orders
that the Red Lion Inn be demolished so that its site might be incorporated in the park and the view in consequence improved. In
the following year his neighbour William Egerton, a member of
Parliament, likewise anxious to enhance the beauty of his grounds,
consulted the landscape gardener Humphry Repton, who advised
him to plant an avenue opening out on to the main road to Knutsford. To achieve this it was necessary to demolish a few poor
cottages, and to rebuild them in a uniform style as 'tenements' on
the same site. A few years earlier, in 1785, at Milton Abbey in
Dorset, Lord Dorchester had had the old hamlet demolished and
removed to a site where it was hidden, by a slope planted with
trees, from the eyes of its noble owner. In fact he took the opportunity to build a model village; forty cottages grouped in pairs,
thatched, and designed to house two families—each comprising a
kitchen and wash-house with a larder on the ground floor and two
gabled rooms on the first floor. The houses were separated by chest-
nut trees, and behind each grew a small garden with passageways
between the houses. In the centre of the village stood a church in
the perpendicular style, the vicarage, the school, almshouses and

a well. Occasionally, as it appears, these autocrats used their authority in 'enlightened' ways, and such influence upon the little world which revolved around them was no less effective. But their absolute authority as expressed in the colossal houses mentioned above had already begun to wane.

THE ARISTOCRATIC IDEAL DECLINES

The architectural ideal known as Palladian, because it was inspired by the work of the Italian *Palladio*, exemplified in stone the conception of the special way of life enjoyed by this class. It expressed certainty in its own supremacy, faith in the exclusiveness of its own leadership, belief in a strict social hierarchy, by virtue of which the principal apartments were raised to a superior height aptly termed 'the noble plan' (the servants being relegated to the semi-basement); a majestic ideal to demonstrate first and foremost the outward signs of power. With the reign of George III this conception began to weaken in architecture as in politics; the Whig ideal was gradually to lose its force.

In 1759 at the onset of this change the building of Harewood House (in Yorkshire) was an indication of new ways. The old house had been purchased in 1753 by Henry Lascelles, director of the East India Company, whose wife was a rich heiress from Barbados in the British West Indies. The Lascelles family were Whig supporters, and Henry's son, Edwin, made up his mind to build in the Palladian style, which was also favoured by the Marquis of Rockingham at nearby Wentworth Woodhouse. His choice is largely explained by the fact that Rockingham was leader of an important group of Whig politicians, and that Edwin as member of Parliament was constantly in the company of this group until, in 1783, he finally joined Pitt. Both Harewood House and Wentworth Woodhouse had indeed been inspired by a very notable earlier building at Wanstead in Essex, built early in the century by the great Whig financier, Sir Richard Childe.

And yet there were conspicuous differences between Wentworth Woodhouse and Harewood; while Wentworth Woodhouse with its façade of 606 feet was an extended Wanstead (only 240 feet), Harewood was constructed to an earlier plan for Wanstead which provided for a façade of 260 feet, now reduced to 240 feet. These diminished proportions of the final edifice appear negligible

23

enough, but the revelation of the desire to *lessen* the proportions was new in itself, since, during the previous reigns, the impulse behind this sort of house had been to build larger and always larger. In the case of Harewood this curtailment resulted in Robert Adam's design, featuring long and numerous corridors, being turned down in favour of a plan by a local architect, John Carr, which made better use of internal space. In this sense, also, Harewood House showed a new trend.

This desire for change was expressed in different form at a slightly later date at Claremont in Surrey. The earlier house, at some time reconstructed by Vanbrugh, had been bought from the Duchess of Newcastle by Robert Clive, who, returning from India, had the house converted by the landscape gardener 'Capability' Brown between 1770 and 1774. The relative simplicity and modesty of his new home served to emphasize the fame Clive had achieved and the immense fortune he had amassed. In fact, the conception was elegant rather than grand, and—a thing still almost unknown—the house contained not only banqueting-rooms, but also water-closets, a powdering-room and even a bathroom under the flight of steps at the south portico (albeit for cold baths only).

Another example of the new trend was Heaton Hall near Manchester. Built in 1772 for Sir Thomas Egerton, first Earl of Wilton, the influence of Kedleston (erected in Derbyshire for Sir Nathaniel Curzon—later Lord Scarsdale) is plainly seen. And yet the two structures belong clearly to separate periods. Kedleston, with its monumental façade (350 feet), its base of rusticated arches, upon which, as at Wanstead, rests the *piano-nobile* with the kitchens behind the colonnade, is one of the most characteristic of all examples of the Palladian concept. At Heaton Hall the façade is reduced to 288 feet, and the arcaded base is replaced by a simple plinth only $2\frac{1}{2}$ feet high, thus doing away with the 'noble plan' and obliging the architect to site the kitchens at the same level as the main rooms. We are not here invited to detect any nuance of a new-found equality between master and man! From now on many new houses were to contain the kitchens on the same floor as the core of the central construction, but still no less essentially kept as far as possible away from the main appartments—often in separate wings—which might on occasion be linked with the central part of the house by tunnels lined with rails for carrying the dishes, as at Doddington Hall in Cheshire, built between 1776 and 1798 by the Reverend Sir Thomas Broughton.

Claremont, Heaton Hall, Doddington Hall and many others are by no means isolated examples. The number of country houses put up during the reign of George III actually equalled the number erected in the whole course of the two previous reigns. What is more, these new houses were no less expensive and luxurious than before. And yet the century of the great Whig mansion, raised to the glory of an autocratic oligarchy, had come to an end. In the design of a country house the concept of a *villa*—that is to say of a building in which emphasis was laid not upon the outside measurements, but rather upon the interior lay-out and its decoration and furnishing—was slowly creeping in, to triumph in due course. When one considers Osterley Park and Syon House near London, the two finest works of the brothers Adam, those pioneers of the new style, it is clear that the original exteriors of the two houses, one Elizabethan and the other Jacobean, were not substantially altered. From 1760 onwards the great stately homes were beginning to become less fashionable, and after 1780 would altogether cease to be so; from now on these vast buildings would be regarded as clumsy legacies of the past. Like the villa, the country house must first and foremost look elegant and be convenient and compact.

Not that the great landowners were short of money—the reign of George III was a time of growing prosperity for the upper class and many members of the middle class, as well as being an era of expansion in industry, trade and colonization. But the middle classes preferred comfort and looked for elegance rather than for the spectacular magnificence and vast display of the old aristocratic homes, and these prosperous middle-class preferences gradually filtered into the mind of the aristocracy. Even the word *villa* became increasingly fashionable, since it succeeded in lending an aura of distinction to those houses insufficiently grand to stand merely on the merits of their dimensions. Tyringham in Buckinghamshire, which was built between 1793 and 1800 by Sir John Soane for the banker William Praed, is the perfect example of these new buildings—both compact and original, wherein the professional architect (a rare being in the era of the great Whig mansion), might modify, invent, and, in his search for new arrangements, not be afraid to reach back into the

'Gothic' past of England or, more exotically, to borrow themes from China, from India, and indeed from France—all in order to reproduce in England medieval castles, Italianate villas or Parisian 'hôtels' (or town-houses).

FURNITURE

In England the successive different styles of furniture before the Hanoverian dynasty were distinguished, as in France, by the names of the monarchs in whose reigns they evolved and became dominant—Elizabethan, Jacobean and Queen Anne. But from 1714 onwards such styles came to be called after their designers, whether famous (like Chippendale) or unknown (like Sheraton), sometimes after the architect (like Adam), or even after amateurs (like Hope) and so on. This change, for what it is worth, was not, as is sometimes believed, due to an especially English traditionalism, causing craftsmen of a later reign to continue manufacturing furniture in the style of the preceding reign, for the practice was not confined to England; in France, for example, in circles at a distance from the Court and in the countryside, craftsmen would sometimes still design a table in the style of Louis XIII, although perfectly aware that the accession of Louis XIV had marked a new era.

The English terms employed under the first three Georges tend, as I see it, to reflect the fact that under the Hanoverians the English Court no longer exerted sufficient influence, or held enough prestige, to impose its own name and style upon fashion in furniture. This is why such terms as Chippendale, Hepplewhite or Sheraton, still in use today, do not in any way correspond with the reigns of the Teutonic kings. When George III came to the throne in 1760 the furniture of the cabinetmaker Chippendale had already been in fashion for several years; in 1754 the latter had produced *The Gentleman and Cabinetmaker's Director,* containing sketches of furniture together with their working drawings. Not all the sketches were by Chippendale, and certain of his larger and better-known pieces, such as his three-legged circular table or his card-table, do not appear in the book. This inventory, like others of the same kind put out to win publicity, laid the emphasis on the novelties, ignoring familiar styles. Nevertheless, the publication of the book was an historical event; from now on works like these, rather than the personal taste of the monarch, were to set the fashions in furniture. The sociological developments represented by these publications in matters of furnishing were comparable to those in the field of literature, in which the aristocrat-patron was being replaced by the publisher. Remarkably enough Chippendale's *Director* of 1754 appeared only a short time before the publication, in February 1755, of Doctor Johnson's famous letter to Lord Chesterfield, which so brilliantly marked the end of the role of the patron in literature. The influential lead in artistic and literary creation from now on was to come from men in business—furniture dealers, picture dealers, booksellers—no longer from the monarch or his courtiers. Here, as in so many other ways, the England of George III was ahead of the rest of the world in economic and social development. In trade Chippendale's *Director* was the forerunner of the modern catalogue.

The *Director*'s success was a sign of the times. As early as 1762 a third edition was called for, while the firm of Ince and Mayhew brought out its own catalogue during the period 1759–63 under the title, *The Universal System of Household Furniture*. The interest which these catalogues aroused was such that in 1788 Thomas Shearer's *Inventory of London Cabinetmakers' Prices, Drawings of Domestic Furniture, The Cabinetmaker and Upholsterer's Drawing Book*, and Hepplewhite's compilation, *The Cabinet and Upholsterer's Guide*, were all published at the same time. Rather later, between 1791 and 1794, it was Sheraton's turn to bring out in instalments *The Cabinetmaker and Upholsterer's Drawing Book*, followed in 1803 by *The Cabinet Dictionary*. While in 1807 Thomas Hope publicized the style which bears his name with a volume entitled *Designs for Household Furniture and Interior Decoration*.

Nowadays antique dealers are in the habit of indicating the various styles of furniture they sell under the names of Chippendale, Hepplewhite, Sheraton and Hope. The last of these names is undoubtedly the only truly accurate one, since it is the only one which may be applied to a specific style. Furthermore, historians came to connect the 'styles' of Chippendale, Hepplewhite and Sheraton with certain well-defined periods. But the favoured dates are on the whole too rigid. It is quite true that these three names are generally thought to have succeeded each other in the above-mentioned order between 1750 and 1800, but it is still necessary when we make use of them to bear in mind the following facts.

No single article of furniture, so far as we know, has ever been identified for certain as the work of Hepplewhite. We know very little of his life, but we do know that his reputation as a cabinet-maker was of no great importance. We know that Sheraton died in poverty, but it is not even certain that he possessed a workshop of his own. Of these three cabinetmakers whose names today are appended to certain styles the only one with a big reputation in his own lifetime was Thomas Chippendale. Even so it is difficult to talk of a Chippendale *style*: some of his pieces were influenced by Adam, others affected the Chinese or Gothic manner; many, indeed, represent an often complicated and not always happy version of the style of Louis XV. In the same way the Sheraton and Hepplewhite styles often recall the French style of Louis XVI, while Regency and Hope are English versions, sometimes made lighter, sometimes heavier, of the Directoire and Empire styles. In this connection it should always be remembered that under George III England was constantly importing French furniture: in 1769 Chippendale himself was fined for having failed to return an exact valuation of French furniture he had brought into the country. Finally, it is easy to cite many cabinetmakers whose reputations stood far higher than those of Hepplewhite and Sheraton: William Vile and John Cobb, Ince and Mayhew, William Gates, John Linnell, William Marsh and Thomas Tatham—others too. The influence of the architect brothers Adam was probably the most important of all.

Robert Adam was one of the men who helped the English to assimilate a Graeco-Roman or neo-classical influence, less austere than the Palladian, which was then emerging in different forms elsewhere in Europe. His *Works in Architecture*, published in 1773, exerted wide influence. One of the happier features of this influence was an ordered attempt to strike a harmony between architecture and interior decoration, including furniture.[1] Adam, who did all his work for the upper classes, consulted well-known cabinetmakers—not only Chippendale, but also Beckwith, Linnell, Norman Seddon, as well as a number of Frenchmen, in the manufacture of his furniture.

---

[1] This search for harmonious effects is in sharp contrast with the individualism expressed by Richard Payne Knight, whose fortified castle at Downton in Herefordshire, combined a 'Gothic' exterior with an interior decorated in the Graeco-Roman manner.

Adam's style, distinguished by lightness, grace and imagination, was a very free, occasionally feminine interpretation of the classical —favouring the Greek, or even the quasi-Hellenistic, rather than the Roman. It was the search for a 'masculine' style, the Roman, in harmony with the ideals of the French Revolution, which led to the reaction against the Adam manner, from henceforth deemed too fragile and effeminate. One of the main exponents of this reaction was the architect Henry Holland, whose work reflected the francophile feeling of the Whig entourage of the Prince of Wales at that time. It was wholly characteristic for Holland to consult French cabinetmakers when he was furnishing Carlton House, the residence of the future George IV. The term 'Regency', which was applied to this new taste in furnishing, should not, however, be interpreted in strictly chronological terms: in the first place Holland died in 1806, that is to say four years before the Regency was officially proclaimed; secondly, the reaction against the Adam style had already shown itself fifteen years before. But the term is just in that it expressed the importance of the personality and the entourage of the Regent in the field of the arts; he was giving his name to the furnishing of the houses of the ruling classes.

While the styles of English furniture under George III are unrelated to those then in fashion on the continent of Europe, yet in the use of materials the period is especially interesting for the more frequent and extensive employment of exotic woods, in particular of American timber, which, after 1770, was allowed into the country free of excise. Thus the value of imported mahogany rose from £30,000 in 1750 to £80,000 in 1792. From the beginning of the reign mahogany from Cuba had become more popular than the San Domingo variety, being softer and easier to work with; later on there was an even greater demand for mahogany from Honduras which was lighter in colour and texture. While mahogany was always used for bedroom furniture and in the dining-room and library, satinwood imported from the West Indies and from India was greatly sought after for use in the drawing-room and boudoir, and after 1800 was much in vogue.

Also under the reign of George III there was a growing demand for particular items of furniture, such as the chest of drawers and library table. This no doubt was due to an increasing taste for the visual arts: such pieces of furniture still left hanging space for pictures and drawings on the walls. The sideboard, containing pots to relieve the stomachs of guests who had eaten and drunk too well, became an integral part of dining-room furnishing. Elsewhere the increase in travel meant that more portable tables and folding beds were being made, and the washstand made its appearance shortly after the accession of George III, together with the shaving-table and its accompanying looking-glass. The shaving-table, according to the catalogues of Shearer and Hepplewhite, also contained the article whose use has been forgotten in present-day England—the bidet.

The dressing-table was more than essential because of the rarity, even in great houses, of bathrooms. Should we perhaps conclude that contemporary authors generally omit any mention of the bathroom through an excess of discretion? The fact remains that the bathroom is scarcely ever mentioned in the descriptions which have remained to us of houses of the aristocracy; the bathroom of the Earl of Leicester at Holkham, for example, is pointed out as an object worthy of note.

On the subject of water-closets contemporary writers are even less articulate. It was rare to find one inside a home. Privies were usually outside the house in what was referred to familiarly as the 'boghouse'. Where a closet did exist in mansions such as Kedleston or Osterley it was unique of its kind, and the very fact of its existence seems important enough to be worthy of mention by contemporary authors. In this again Holkham was undoubtedly one of the most favoured houses. Not only had William Kent endowed it with a lavatory in a corner of the hall, but this lavatory was double-seated. However, the reign of George III was particularly notable for important technical improvements in the matter of human waste disposal. In fact, the first patents for ballcock and water-closets—the 'Ajax' of Alexander and the 'Bramah' of Joseph Bramah—were the real forerunners of the modern water-closet.

LANDSCAPE AND GARDENS

The grounds surrounding the house were frequently at least as important as the building itself. But here we must clarify the meaning of the terms 'garden' and 'gardening', as earlier we clarified the word 'country house', for in each case we are dealing with typically English terms. The great aristocrat loved to gaze from his window over a vast expanse of lawns, trees and water. By 'gardening' was implied the artificial contriving of gracious and imposing landscape composition. Nowadays the word has degenerated: it applies to what is no more than a branch of horticulture. The change of meaning was gradually effected in the early years of the nineteenth century. As late as 1809, when Walter Nicol published his thesis on gardening in the modern sense of the word, he entitled his book *Town and Villa Gardens*, hoping to avoid confusion. In the eighteenth century any flowers that were allowed to grow were usually confined to a walled plot or 'flower garden', which, like the kitchen garden with its vegetables, was invisible from the house.

Trees rather than flowers were the important feature of eighteenth-century grounds. They served as screens to conceal unattractive objects, to protect the house itself from prying eyes. Later, towards the turn of the century, even the ordinary vicarage made use of trees in this way. Jane Austen describes how one parson planted trees to hide the cemetery, and another to remove from his sight a farm and the blacksmith's forge. Ironically enough, the great landowners in Jane Austen's actual world planted trees so that they might not have to see the vicarage. 'Capability' Brown advised the Honourable Thomas Clifford at his seat at Tixall in Staffordshire to plant in order to preserve his view.

Lancelot Brown very soon acquired the nickname 'Capability' because of his readiness to assess the 'possibilities' or 'capabilities' (a more euphonious word) for improvement latent in the landscapes his rich clients laid before him. In the beginning of the reign Capability was forty-four years of age and had already spent ten years transforming the pleasure grounds of the great English mansions. He continued to do so until his death in 1783. Staffordshire was one of the counties in which he achieved his biggest impact, in the grounds of seven or eight noble houses within a radius of twenty-four miles. But he also worked in Wiltshire and Hampshire; indeed, there was scarcely a district in which he did not leave his mark. Brown was particularly interested in park landscapes, the bounds of which he generally defined by planting an irregular belt of trees. By the end of the century Repton's admirers were accusing Brown of having 'deforested' the English countryside. Indeed Brown felled trees (as Repton himself later did) wherever he believed it essential to the provision of an unrestricted view. Whereas Repton made use of trees in great numbers, Brown planted them in clumps within the grounds themselves; but it is gross exaggeration to talk of 'deforestation'. It is more correct to say that Brown planted less indiscriminately than Repton.

From 1788 Humphrey Repton, who came from a well-to-do background (while Brown came of humble parentage), worked as Brown had done to beautify the grounds and houses of the aristocracy, until he was forced, on account of a carriage accident sustained in 1811, to lead a very much less active life. His influence extended not only over the southern counties of England, but up to the Yorkshire borders, as well as over the east and west of the country. Fashion and the controversy of the time tended to exaggerate the contrast between the works of Brown and Repton. Looking back, it would seem more correct to state that Repton extended, emphasized and enlarged upon the ideas already developed by Brown. His definition of a park as the areas of wood and lawn seen from the windows of a house, is intrinsically Brown's. But Repton contributed one genuine innovation; he laid down the absolute rule by which this part of the grounds should appear to have no bounds. From this arose the idea of contriving terraces in the immediate neighbourhood of the house to extend the view as far as possible into the horizon. From it too arose the abundant use of trees designed to avoid too sharp a contrast between the park and the neighbouring rural countryside. Repton for instance, advised his clients to graze their cows in the most distant areas of the park. Furthermore, as we have already remarked, the latter brought into fashion the lavish use of plantations. Thus for example, Lord Weymouth at Longleat put in almost 50,000 trees; while at Corsham Court Repton planted 4,500 oaks of various species, 1,550 chestnuts, 1,450 beeches, 600 elms, and a hundred sycamores. Some great landowners, however, followed the Duke of Argyll's example, and planted exotic species imported from the West Indies or the Americas. Towards the end of the reign Beckford at Fonthill boasted that he had arranged for one million plants to be imported from America. The author of *Vathek* perhaps allowed himself some license as to exact numbers, but today we may still marvel at the variety of American species at Fonthill, some of which have grown to gigantic proportions.

Brown had already understood the importance of water. He had dammed a small river at Blenheim for the fourth Duke of Marlborough, from which he proceeded to form two lakes excellently in keeping with the proportions of the palace. For the fourth Duke of Devonshire at Chatsworth he had banked up a river and made it more conspicuous by the levelling of the adjoining land. At Fisherwick in Staffordshire he had again dammed up a river, this time to provide a waterfall. For Lord Bute at Luton Hoo he had created an artificial lake and embellished it with small wooded islets. At Wimpole Hall, Cambridgeshire, for the Lord Chancellor, Lord Hardwicke, Brown transformed a little group of ponds into two lakes, complete with bridges—one for utility and one for ornament. And since Lord Hardwicke had already improved his view with a mock ruin of a castle, Brown constructed within the ruin an actual dwelling which served to house a number of servants.

And so throughout the reign the landscapes were ornamented with mock castles, mock ruins, sham bridges and artificial rivers; there were grottoes and hermitages contrived among rocks, sometimes, if the proprietor was intent on complete verisimilitude, inhabited by a hermit hired for the job. Brown was generally willing to design utilitarian buildings, but in a style more in keeping with the bizarre than with the main house; a menagerie for example, in the form of an elegant Ionic rotunda, and, at Castle Ashby, a dairy in the shape of a Greek temple. For Broadlands he designed an orangery; for Corsham Court an enchanting neo-Gothic-cum-Moorish bathing-pool—the 'bath-house'—as well as other exotica. Later, through Repton's work, the thatched cottage became fashionable, its smoke curling mournfully into the sky to complete and embellish the view.

COSTUME

When the first two Georges had come to the throne—one in 1714, the second in 1727—they were both forty-four years old. And therefore, until the accession of George III in 1760, fashions in masculine dress were primarily designed for men of this sort of age. But in 1760 George III was only twenty-two, and so from then on fashion was centred upon young men in their twenties. When George III in due course attained the age of forty-four, the Prince of Wales was twenty and male fashion revolved once more around his age group.

Up to 1780–85 masculine fashion in elegant society had reached extravagant proportions; this was the splendid era of the 'macaroni'

c

with his enormous wig, his shoes fastened with great buckles, in fact with every feature of his clothing 'redolent', as the Prussian pastor Moritz remarked, of 'francification'. But after the Prince of Wales came of age in 1782, a new tendency began to creep in, encouraged by the Prince's friends with Charles James Fox in the lead. Now casual dress was all the rage; men wore their own hair instead of a wig over a shorn head, as had earlier been the custom. Above all the man's coat, erstwhile close-fitting, was replaced by a loose coat—the 'frock' coat—copied from the lower classes. At first reserved for ordinary everyday wear, eventually its use became widespread except at Court and on ceremonial occasions. But the French Revolution accelerated the movement towards greater simplicity: the tax levied by Pitt upon wig powder in 1795 succeeded in banishing this accessory; only lawyers, or older men wishing to conceal their baldness, still retained it. Lace cuffs were no longer worn, laces replaced shoe buckles, while trousers gradually ousted the former breeches which after a time were worn only on ceremonial occasions. The tricorn hat, in universal use throughout the reign, gradually gave way to a high rounded shape. One contemporary writer, referring to masculine attire, remarked: 'this is the day of Jacobinism and of equality'. Reaction against the casual attitude of the revolutionary era was not to set in until George ('Beau') Brummel—the 'Napoleon of dress'. And even then there was to be no reversal of the triumph of simplicity.

The evolution of female dress was similar. While, at the start of the century, women's clothes had been designed for the woman of thirty, after 1760 designs became progressively younger, until in the last twenty years of the reign they were intended for the girl of seventeen—a trend reaching its peak with the regency dress, its virginal whiteness symbolizing the ideal of feminine fashion. Until 1793 Marie Antoinette was the Englishwoman's ideal model; the favourite material of the well-dressed woman was French silk, a fashion which endured for many years, until after the French Revolution silk lost its place to imported Indian cotton.

Even before the Revolution the figure had begun to change. Hoops, so fashionable during the first twenty years of the reign, disappeared between 1780 and 1790. Furthermore, until about 1770 well-dressed women wore only two styles of dress—fastened from the top to the hem, or open to allow a glimpse of an embroidered skirt in front. Between 1770 and 1780 the bodice and

skirt—copied from a lower strata of society, and at first worn as
negligée or morning wear, appeared on other occasions. The
bodices of dresses worn on formal occasions remained very *décolleté*, moving ever lower, for the bosom throughout the reign represented the erogenous zone *par excellence*. It is significant that
novelists of the eighteenth century were more inclined to describe
the heroine's bosom than her face, and that beguiling heroines
captivated men with glimpses of white throats. Those who were
less than well endowed in this respect often made use of 'bosom
friends',[1] which at least on public appearances gave an illusion of
curves. Indeed, until 1790 women used false rumps, false bottoms,
and pads of every sort. But between 1790–93 these 'advantages'
disappeared: the time had come for 'return to nature', for a 'revolutionary simplicity': beneath a close-fitting cotton dress there was
room for only the very slightest of under-garments; shifts and petti-
coats were of the barest; short drawers became miniscule, and sometimes disappeared altogether—a favourite subject for cartoonists
when in a high wind dresses flew up easily. In winter as in summer
muslin was fashionable—so diaphanous that it displayed the figure
in detail. In 1806 women adopted a chemise dress with its high
belt supporting the bosom and accentuating its curves while the
décolleté—now lower than ever—left little of the breasts concealed.
Bare arms came into fashion until the advent, with the 'Gothic'
renaissance, of 'slashed' sleeves. Dresses became shorter, revealing
the shape of the leg and inspiring the poet to this sort of verse:

> White-muslined misses and mammas are seen,
> Linked with gay cockneys, glittering o'er the green:
> The rising breeze unnumbered charms displays,
> And the tight ankle strikes the astonished gaze.

During the 1770s and into the '80s, elegant women as well as
men had reached the height of absurdity in the dressing of hair:
heaps of false hair decorated with flowers, vegetables or ostrich
feathers, were raised into high edifices, and kept in place by much
pomading—the whole lavishly powdered with flour. The structure
was so complicated that it was not taken down at night but merely
tied into a bag. A mouse lodged itself in Mrs Coke's hairbag (she
was the wife of the famous farmer, Thomas Coke, of whom we shall
hear later), and terrified that lady so much that she miscarried.

[1] A lace-edged handkerchief used to fill in a *décolleté*.

35

The French Revolution put an end once and for all to such extravagances, which had in any case since 1780 begun to decline.

Indeed the return to simplicity in itself gave rise to a few 'excesses', to judge from the names of certain fashionable styles of hairdressing: after 1793 hair *'à la victime'* and *'à la guillotine'* was favoured. But this sort of thing was rare and of short duration; natural curls soon found favour again among elegant women.

EVERYDAY LIFE AND CUSTOMS

The French traveller, Faujas de Saint-Fond, described a day spent as guest in an English country house towards the end of the eighteenth century. At ten o'clock a bell was rung for breakfast.

' . . . We then repair to a large room ornamented with historical pictures of the family; here we find several tables, covered with tea-kettles, fresh cream, excellent butter, rolls of several kinds, and in the midst of all bouquets of flowers, newspapers and books. There are besides, in this room a billiard-table, pianos and other musical instruments.

'After breakfast, some walk in the parks, others employ themselves in reading or in music, or return to their rooms until half-past four, when the bell makes itself heard to announce that dinner is ready; we all go to the dining-room where the table is usually laid for twenty-five or thirty covers. When every one is seated, the chaplain according to custom makes a short prayer and blesses the food, which is eaten with pleasure, for the dishes are prepared after the manner of an excellent French cook; everything is served here as in Paris, except some courses in the English style, for which a certain predilection is preserved; but this makes a variety, and thus gives the epicures of every country an opportunity of pleasing their palates.'

Faujas de Saint-Fond goes on to describe English tableforks, which he disliked, since they 'prick my mouth or my tongue with their little sharp steel tridents'. These 'tridents' were not handled as in France; indeed, in England the small fork 'is always held in the left hand and the knife in the right. The fork seizes, the knife cuts, and the pieces may be carried to the mouth with either. The motion is quick and precise. The manœuvres at an English dinner are founded upon the same principle as the Prussian tactics—not

a moment is lost'. And, Faujas concludes: 'The English plan is better, but it necessitates large blunt knives rounded at the point. Well, what harm was there in that? It would mean one weapon less in the hands of fools or villains'.
This aristocratic board held:

'. . . entrées, the rôti, the entremets . . . all served as in France with the same variety and abundance. If the poultry be not so juicy as in Paris, one eats here in compensation hazelhens, and above all moorfowl, delicious fish . . . at the dessert the scene changes; the cloth, the napkins and everything vanish. The mahogany table appears in all its lustre; but is soon covered with brilliant decanters, filled with the best wines; comfits, in fine porcelain or crystal vases; and fruits of different kinds in elegant baskets. Plates are distributed together with many glasses, and in every object elegance and convenience seem to rival each other. Towards the end of the dessert, the ladies withdraw to a room destined for the teatable . . .'

The gallant Frenchman felt 'that they are left alone a little too long' However, he agrees that their presence might have been awkward during the ceremony of toasts', since 'If the lively champagne should make its diuretic influence felt, the case is foreseen, and in the pretty corners of the room the necessary convenience is to be found. This is applied to with so little ceremony that the person who has occasion to use it does not even interrupt his talk during the operation.'

The guests then proceed to the drawing-room 'where tea and coffee abound, and where the ladies do the honours of the table with much grace and ceremony; the tea is always excellent, but it is not so with the coffee'. Indeed, if Faujas is to be believed 'the English attach no importance to the perfume and flavour of good coffee; for it seems to be all one to them what kind they drink, provided they have four or five cupfuls of it. Their coffee is always weak and bitter, and has completely lost its aromatic flavour.' After this 'those who wished retire to their rooms; those who prefer conversation or music remain in the drawing-room; others go out for a walk. At ten o'clock supper is served and those who please attend it. I find that as a rule people eat a great deal more in England than in France'. This was true of the upper classes, at least.

Another peculiarity of this class was the freedom of manners it enjoyed. In 1784, another Frenchman, François de la Rochefoucauld, travelling in England, was dumbfounded by the casual behaviour of young men in high society: 'they hum under their breath, they whistle, they sit down in a large armchair and put their feet on another, they sit on any table in the room and do a thousand other things which would be quite ridiculous in France, but are done quite naturally in England'. And la Rochefoucauld felt that 'it would be impossible to be more easy-going in good society than one is in England'. Such indifference to the conventions was not just the privilege of youth. When this traveller, bearing a letter of introduction, called upon Sir Gerard Vanneck, Baronet, member of Parliament, business magnate and London banker (these attributes and functions were typical of the new landed gentry to which he belonged), his host, who was forty-one, welcomed him to his magnificent stately home—Heveningham Hall in Suffolk. 'He received us very coldly, and, with his hat still on, invited us to enter.' But la Rochefoucauld was not put out: 'no notice should be taken of this kind of thing in England. The goodwill is there; it is merely the form that is lacking. We retired to put on our own hats and then entered'. And, since Sir Gerard's sister was eating breakfast, all in the same informal manner the stranger was invited to share it with her; the conversation became 'less chilly every minute', and la Rochefoucauld perceived that off-hand manners did not preclude the warmest show of hospitality.

The description which Faujas de Saint-Fond has written of his day with the aristocracy should not encourage us to think that every landowner led so idle an existence in his mansion, the background of English countryside serving to enhance an ostentatious way of life. It is true that few of these landowners actually worked their own land; they allowed their tenants to farm it: at the most they cultivated a small fraction of their estate themselves. But it would be too sweeping to conclude that they were not concerned in the farming of their acres; they were interested, if for no better reason than that it was the fashion to be so, or because many of them understood that the more efficient the cultivation, then the higher would prove the yield, and therefore the figure of the rent to be exacted. This is a point which emerges with some force in the writings of Arthur Young. In 1768, from publications in which he described rural conditions in the different regions of England, we can understand the interest he helped to arouse among the upper classes, by the way in which he demonstrated that intelligent cultivation of the land, supported by generous capital expenditure, can provide considerable profits. The sovereign himself gave some unexpectedly impressive leads in this field, beginning personally to cultivate the royal estate at Windsor, where in 1765 he set up two model farms—one in the Flemish, the other in the Norfolk style. This action achieved two things—first it served to increase the popularity of George III, and in addition it brought agriculture into a limelight it had not enjoyed since the day of Pope and Sir Robert Walpole. The Whig aristocracy nick-named him 'Farmer George', and he and his flock of merino sheep became symbolic figures.

Another powerful and important image, who contributed more than anyone to the popularity of agriculture, was paradoxically a determined and austere Whig, Thomas Coke of Norfolk, a man gifted, according to Doctor Johnson with a good deal of 'malevolence'. The editor of *The Times* was perhaps too fulsome in his praise: 'He did more for agriculture than any other Englishman, perhaps more than any other human being'. It has with some truth been said that development of the area lying between Lynn and Holkham, and often attributed to Coke's organization, had begun at an earlier date. There is, however, no reason to question the undoubted contribution he made in kind by investing £500,000 in land improvement, whose value, thanks to the use of marling, had increased. Holkham, which in 1776 produced a revenue of £2,200, in 1816 was providing £20,000. He had also succeeded in improving his stock by use of controlled feeding, through selective breeding and land improvement. He experimented with new methods of cultivation from which he adopted the most profitable. Finally he erected for his tenant farmers, farm buildings and dwelling-houses which set a standard to neighbouring landowners. Thomas Coke would rise as early as his labourers, and dressed in an ordinary smock he tilled the land at their side.

Not every great landowner was so methodical in the use of new techniques; but there was one great politician and aristocrat, the Marquis of Rockingham, who did not confine his interest to Wentworth Woodhouse, the splendid mansion which we mentioned earlier; he retained two thousand acres to his own use, on which he organized experiments in the use of fertilizers and in soil improvement. The Duke of Norfolk, too, was experimenting in new techniques with carrots and kale. Lord Milton and the Earl of Albemarle were specializing in the cultivation of sainfoin.

This is not to say that progress in agriculture under George III was achieved solely through the inspired activity of a variety of advanced amateurs . . . but the interest they showed in farming as a branch of the economy was an encouragement to farmers, and helped to induce a feeling of interest in research, and new findings in agriculture. But their personal action was limited in its scope and its immediate effects. The efforts of the larger farmers, whose cultivation was often spread over many hundreds of acres, may not have attracted the same attention. But although less publicized, their influence in regard to the adoption of new techniques was no less positive.

THE LARGER FARMS

Certain counties in the eighteenth century were reputed for the farms they contained; these were farms where the 'open field' system of cultivation, which had divided the land into strips, had been universally abandoned, and where obligatory exchange and concentration of the land through the system of 'enclosure' had progressed furthest, the whole process having been speeded up towards the end of the previous reign. Hertfordshire, Essex and Suffolk, together with Norfolk and Leicestershire were considered the more prosperous of the agricultural counties. At the beginning of the reign of George III, Hertfordshire led the way, to be replaced at the close by Norfolk.

In 1784 François de la Rochefoucauld visited one of the larger Suffolk farms—the property of a high-ranking civil servant, Francis Hale Rigby, the Paymaster General—whose acres, la Rochefoucauld tells us, yielded £7 to £800 a year. The visitor was impressed by the elegance of the farm-house, which was

'. . . more like a gentleman's house than a farmer's; it is a two-storey house built in brick with string-courses of stone; it has five windows on each front and at one end a little turret which the English call a "bow", forming one of those sitting-rooms which are so common in England. In front of the house is a well-kept lawn, surrounded by green trees, which comes right up to the door of the house. Behind the house are the usual farm buildings—barns, a stable and so on. They are built of boards joined together and painted brown, the whole being roofed with thatch. This type of building is very common and, I imagine, the cheapest; it lasts a long time. The boards are generally of fir or pine and are preserved by their own resin and a coat of paint.'

On the same journey to England, this time through Norfolk, la Rochefoucauld visited a farmer whose house stood in the centre of an area of about 400 acres. He describes it to us:

'The farmhouse is attractive and extremely clean; there are no costly objects to be seen, nothing that one would describe as luxury . . . Behind the farmer's house is a little vegetable-garden, and a little farther on a small wood wholly designed to suit his [the farmer's] own taste; a number of little walks and pleasant prospects give it a considerable charm.'

The farmer was a young man named Curtis, who impressed the stranger with his politeness and prepossessing appearance: 'He has a large income of his own, and is one of the leading fox-hunters in the whole county. He always keeps two or three hunters, one of which cost him a hundred guineas; for a painting of this horse, which I saw, he paid twenty guineas.' As la Rochefoucauld remarks —a very rich farmer. The small farmer's way of life was quite different, nearer to the life of his own labourers.

CHAPTER TWO

THE MIDDLE AND LOWER CLASSES

HOUSING

Somewhere between the house of the small farmer and the splendid home of the great landowner stood the houses of the small gentry. These generally contained a hall, one or two dining-rooms and seven or eight bedrooms, a study, and more often than not a music room or library. The farmhouse, even if it had only recently been reconstructed, was still more modest, usually comprising a dining-room, bedroom and drawing-room on the ground floor, with a varying number of bedrooms, never more than two or three, up-stairs. The kitchen, larder and dairy, as well as other rooms retained to some specific use, were often found in outhouses behind and adjoining the main building. There were many farmhouses of this type in Sussex. Farmhouses in Essex usually contained six to eight rooms. A few such houses when 'improved' were considered to have been made 'respectable' and fit for 'gentlemen'. The poor peasantry were very differently housed. The naturalist Gilbert White, living in his village of Selborne in Hampshire, declared that in 1789 there were very many poor people who lived '. . . comfortably in good stone or brick cottages which are glazed and have chambers above stairs'. And he emphasized the fact that there were no mud cottages. In other parts of the country the poor were less well provided for: their dwelling consisted for the most part of a single room, two at the most, the floor sometimes flagged, but more often of beaten earth, the door the only access to the outside air. For furniture there might be a bench, one or two chairs, a table and a bed; the children slept most likely on a flock mattress placed directly on the ground.

FOOD

Except where the farmer was undernourished his eating habits were undoubtedly healthier than those of the upper classes, whose over-rich and plentiful food made them constantly prone to attacks

42

of gout. The farmer seldom ate meat, but milk, cereals and an increasing use of vegetables and fruit produced on his own land made up his diet. In certain parts of the country the food of the peasantry, that is of farm servants and labourers, was more or less identical. In the North their diet was based on oatmeal, potatoes, bacon and buttermilk. In the South it consisted, at least at the beginning of the reign, of bread, beef and beer; towards the turn of the century bread had become the staple part of the meal, and beef had disappeared to be replaced by a small piece of bacon on Saturdays and Sundays, and this, with an occasional piece of very hard cheese made from skimmed milk, completed the diet. In the Midlands many agricultural workers lived on barley or rye bread and potatoes. Tea was coming to replace beer, and skim-milk was drunk instead of milk, particularly amongst the poorer families where enclosure of the open fields prevented them from keeping their own cow. The English peasant liked his tea strong, but at the time of the Napoleonic wars the housewife was often obliged to stew the same leaves so often that the drink was both colourless and tasteless. Tea at this time cost 16s a pound.

THE PEASANTRY

While there are numerous accounts of the passions and recreations of high society, not much is known about the lives of the lower classes, and especially of the poorer peasant class. This is why the story of Ann Hurst (which is included by Sir Frederick Morton Eden in his book *The State of the Poor,* published in 1797) is especially valuable.

Ann was born at the beginning of the century; the daughter of a Surrey farmer, she was placed in domestic service as soon as she was able to work. She was not yet twenty when she married one of her fellow employees, James Strudwick, also a day-labourer. For more than sixty years he worked on the same farm for a shilling a day, stopping only seven weeks before his death at the age of eighty in 1787, never having had to rely on relief from the parish. The Strudwicks had seven children and sixteen grandchildren, all of whom became day-labourers like their parents and grandparents before them. Until 1787 Ann provided for the family with the seven shillings which James brought home faithfully each week. She lived on after her husband's death for a further seven years.

43

Despite her age and infirmity she went on working in order to survive, weeding a 'gentleman's' garden for a wage which never rose above 6d a day. It is true that a rich person of charity allowed her the sum of £1 a year after her husband died, and this saved a proud woman from seeking parish relief. When she ordered her husband's coffin she was looked upon askance in her village for extravagance, because she insisted upon a coffin with handles and an inscription with James's age engraved on it; but she was determined to give him, to use her own words, a 'decent' funeral. She made a point of reminding one of his cousins, a mason who on Saturday nights went to drink a tankard of beer at the inn, that James had not spent five shillings on himself during his whole life-time—luckily he had never had so much money in his pocket, she hastened to add. Her one fear as she grew older was that she might be forced to 'fall on the parish', and from time to time in moments of anxiety she took to asking herself whether perhaps the Almighty, in leaving her so long upon earth, had forgotten all about her. Such impious thoughts were severely criticized by her neighbours.

We may add at this point that if to the minds of Sir Frederick Morton Eden and members of his class in general, Ann Strudwick was typical of the peasant class, not all of them possessed her courage and patience. In 1795, for example, contemporary writers from various parts of the country recorded cases of carts on the way to market being held up by housewives, who forced their owners to sell them grain then and there at a deflated price.

It is difficult sometimes to understand how at this period the peasant poet, John Clare, was able to write:

> The milkmaid singing leaves her bed,
> As glad as happy thoughts can be. . . .

And yet, apart from the melancholy periods during the Napoleonic Wars, his lines portrayed the general feeling of those days as described for us by foreign travellers in England.

PROSPERITY IN THE COUNTRYSIDE

In 1765 Monsieur Grosley, a native of Champagne, was amazed by the clothes of the 'labourers and husbandmen' all dressed 'in good cloth, a warm great coat upon his back, and good boots on his legs. . . .' The farmers themselves were: 'well-dressed, well-fed;

and notwithstanding they buy everything at a high price, they live in ease and affluence'. Rural dwellings were 'built of brick and covered with tiles, have glass windows'; surprising to a visitor from France, where walls were of earth, there were plenty of thatched roofs, and where window-panes were a sign of wealth.

In 1788, too, a young Frenchman—who had admittedly travelled only in the Southern counties—declared that he had never seen poverty in England; that all, even the least wealthy inhabitants, were clothed in good cloth. And having in mind the French peasant who often went barefoot, he noticed that English shoes were waterproof.

It is in fact of interest to compare the continental peasant at this date—and the Frenchman was by no means the most unfortunate —with his English cousin, if one is to receive some accurate impression of his standard of living. The French visitor was exaggerating when he affirmed that: 'You never see the English truly assailed by poverty; I mean by this that you do not see the people starving, without clothes or shelter from the weather.' And the picture he paints of England is, generally speaking, a little too good to be true: 'Fine old men standing in the shade of ancient oak-trees, children playing at their feet, as fair and rosy, as beautiful as those of Guido[1] and Albani. . . .'

But the children of the poor never had time to play games, and old men would have to work, often to the day they died.

Nevertheless, on the whole England emerges well from the comparison, since over a large part of the country the development of agriculture, thanks to new techniques and heavy investment of capital, was more advanced than in other lands. As to manners, the Prussian pastor Moritz had echoed the impressions of the visitors from France, and had besides observed other qualities, such as the easy ways of the villagers, the politeness of their children, and the friendliness of the welcome accorded to strangers. The countryside might be poor or prosperous—it varied from one region to another, but the inhabitants usually impressed the visitor with the warmth of their feelings. As in other countries the standard of living varied among individuals and social classes, in proportion to the degree of economic development attained by any given region of the country. But there is no doubt that to the French or German traveller disembarking at Dover or

[1] Guido Reni.

'Brighthelmstone' (our modern Brighton), the journey from the coast to London through the English countryside of Sussex, Surrey and Kent, offered an enchanting glimpse of a new land:

'Go there, exclaimed a young gentleman from Brittany on the eve of the French Revolution. Go by the road I took myself, arriving at sundown, with no preconceptions. See then how men, women, children gather round after the labour of the day, freely plying friends, acquaintances, even casual passers-by, with beer, cakes, punch, while a noisy band of sailors joke with the passengers from half a dozen coaches. Contemplate this rustic scene against a surrounding background of poplars, trees of every kind, little houses overshadowed by the numerous belfries of a great city. Then let the scene be animated by the movements of elegant carriages, horses fleet as deer, the gay clothing of the young people, the amazons riding by, their veils revealing nothing but the whiteness of their skin and their aloofness. Consider this picture and ask yourself whether anywhere in the world there can be a road more various, more beautiful, more picturesque than the highroad from Brighthelmstone to London.'

To the sceptic this would no doubt appear as an idealized picture. But to us it accords very well with the evidence of those admirable documents which are the water colours of the contemporary painter, Thomas Rowlandson.

PART TWO

MONEY AND THE WORLD
OF INDUSTRY

1. Wentworth House

2.

a. John Wilkes

b. Thomas Paine

c. Grace Dalrymple Eliot

d. 'Capability' Brown

CHAPTER ONE

THE LARGER UNDERTAKINGS

The elements of modern industry in England did not come alive under George III. Before 1760 there already existed various types of enterprise, particularly in textiles, and these had the characteristics of business concerns. But with a few rare exceptions the men who ran them were business magnates who purchased the raw materials, gave them out to be worked, sometimes in special premises but more often in individual cottagers' homes, and then collected and distributed the finished products. The large factory or mill, managed by the proprietor of the machines and buildings and giving employment to hundreds of workpeople on a fixed weekly wage, was still the exception. It was only under George III that this type of enterprise became widespread, existing side by side with the small workshop and home industry. In fact, these different systems were to co-exist right through the Industrial Revolution and until the later years of the nineteenth century. Under George III there were cases in Yorkshire, at Wortley or at Huddersfield, for example, where the same cloth merchant employed some workmen in his own mill and others in his own home. There were cutlers in Sheffield who rented a factory-bench where they worked for an employer who did not actually own the factory. In the same way nailers in the 'Black Country' who did not own a forge would rent a factory-bench. It is difficult to believe that even in Birmingham, as late as 1856, most of the workshops employed only five or six workmen.

In the first half of the nineteenth century there was an increase rather than a decline in the number of small factories. And work at home had by no means disappeared. The very terms used to describe a large business betray the vagueness of ideas and the complexity of the industrial changes then taking place. If we study contemporary writings we conclude that terms such as 'manufacture' and 'manufactory' (from which the modern 'factory' is derived) were used indiscriminately, and taken literally refer to

D

buildings where work was done by hand, which was obviously becoming less and less general.

Yet it is interesting to watch the development of one such business which came into being in the eighteenth century and has survived to the present day. Let us take the foundry at Coalbrookdale, which was established by Abraham Darby.

THE IRON-MASTERS OF COALBROOKDALE

John Darby, the father of the founder, was a Worcestershire farmer, and like many other farmers in that part of England he owned a forge where he produced nails and locks in whatever time he took off from his work in the fields; he would drive to the nearest market and sell his wares to the big merchants who then sent them to London. Abraham, his son, in due course set up on his own, first in Bristol in 1699, and then in 1709 at Coalbrookdale in Shropshire. Some time before, aided by an apprentice, John Thomas, he had succeeded in producing cast-iron containers moulded in sand: while these experiments were going on Abraham ensured that the process was kept secret by blocking up the keyhole to prevent curious spies. This detail is not uninteresting since industrial espionage was to increase greatly during the reign with the coming of important inventions. What is more, when his seven years' apprenticeship came to an end John Thomas was offered work with some of Darby's rivals at double the salary he had been receiving: enticement of this sort was used intensively during the period of which we are speaking.

Abraham Darby was also one of the first manufacturers to substitute coke for coal in the forging of iron. But this method did not come into general use until a few months later, in 1783–84 the process of smelting iron ores known as 'puddling', had been discovered by a Welsh foreman and separately by Henry Cort, a supplier to the Admiralty. The results of this discovery spread with unusual rapidity because Cort, who had been made bankrupt through the suicide of one of his creditors, lost the rights of his patent, whereupon his invention at once reverted to public use. The metal industry now forged ahead in importance and became concentrated in the coal-basins of Staffordshire, South Wales, Yorkshire and the Clyde.

The Coalbrookdale Company, meanwhile, was managed through

50

the reign of George III by Abraham II, the son of the first Abraham Darby, until 1763 and thereafter until the end of 1789 by the grandson, Abraham III. The name of Darby was to appear continuously in the list of directors of the firm until the middle of the nineteenth century. And other families during the period were associated with the Darby empire: the Reynolds, the Rathbones, Dickinsons, Dearmans and others. These were all linked with the Darbys by bonds of marriage and religion: for they all belonged to the Society of Friends, better known as Quakers, of whom we shall speak later. The families of Rose, Thomas, Luccock, Norris, Cranage, etc., who were included among the foremen of the Company, were also Quakers, and so were some of the staunchest customers. Furthermore, when the directors travelled about they always chose Quakers with whom to lodge if possible. The Quakers, like other dissenters, suffered for their faith and had come to found a lasting source of human relationships, business and personal, on the community of faith. In any case, for some time past religious meetings had been held in the offices of the Company, not only on Sundays but week-days as well. This community of faith assisted relations between the directors and the workers, some of whom had also come from a Quaker background. For during the whole period of the Industrial Revolution the factory owners were the sole arbiters in matters of working discipline.

The working day began at six in the morning and ended twelve hours later, with half an hour for lunch and an hour for dinner. The rules incorporated a system of fines for absenteeism without good cause, for bringing strong drink to work, for brawling and fighting and so on.

The word 'dynasty', always used in speaking of the Darby family, need not mislead us: the Darbys and the Reynolds (it was Richard Reynolds who in 1767 replaced wooden rails with iron, and substituted the new steam engine invented by Watt for the old Newcomen engine) had no desire, in spite of their success, to live like lords in the way the parvenu Arkwright and even Boulton— 'the iron chieftain'—had done. They did not follow the by now established fashion of building themselves magnificent houses and buying great ancestral homes. Instead they founded schools, erected houses for their workers, laid roads and dug canals, while continuing to live in their modest houses, as close as possible to their works. They lived and died in Coalbrookdale, and were buried

51

there—their tombstones bear only their names and their dates of birth and death.

Yet their business had progressed over the century: if we compare an inventory drawn up in 1718 with a later one of 1810 we can see that the total net value of the ironworks had risen from about £4,200 to more than £164,000. As Matthew Boulton pointed out towards the end of the century, if one wanted to make a living in the metal industry, then it was necessary either to work as a forger oneself, or else to be in possession of a very large fortune. While during the first years of the century it was possible to build and work an iron-foundry like Coalbrookdale with a mere £5,000, eighty years later this figure would need to be multiplied at least tenfold to obtain the same result.

A LARGE IRON FOUNDRY

In 1760 John Roebuck, a doctor, founded at Carron on the Firth of Forth, some thirty-six miles from Edinburgh, a metal industry which was to be a model of its kind. Unfortunately he was unwise enough to dissipate his efforts and divert capital into other enterprises, and in 1773 he became bankrupt. But a group of English and Scots associates refloated the company with sufficient capital—it rose quickly to £150,000—to allow it to run at a profit.

In 1797 the Frenchman Faujas de Saint-Fond expressed a wish to visit the Carron works. He was travelling through Scotland in the company of Count Andreani of Milan and an American, William Thornton. It was impossible to visit the works without 'very strong recommendations', but Faujas was lucky enough to run into a certain Dr Swediaur, well-known to the works management, in an Edinburgh street. Thanks to him the travellers were admitted on their names, titles and addresses alone. One wonders how this ease of access was consistent with the widespread and justifiable fear of industrial espionage. There is, however, no doubt that visits of this kind by distinguished foreigners provided interesting free publicity, besides potentially favourable openings for new markets abroad. In any case the travellers were not allowed to enter the gun-foundry 'which nobody was allowed to see'. It was in here that were made 'those large pieces, short and expanded at the breech, which bear the name of carronades'. According to

52

Faujas, there was some especial secrecy attached to the process of coating the cannon with metal. When the small group of visitors passed the place where these objects were cast, they were told 'very politely' that particular processes and machines unknown to any other establishment of the kind rendered it necessary to keep that place concealed from strangers, whereupon 'we thought this was very reasonable, and followed our conductor to another quarter'.

The visitors soon found themselves among machines of every sort in an unbelievable din: 'the shrill creaking of pulleys, the continued noise of hammers, the activity of those arms which give the impulse to so many machines; everything here presents a spectacle as new as it is interesting'. One of them in particular reminded the visitors of

'. . . the most pleasing ideas . . . they cast boilers five feet in diameter for the making of sugar in the West Indies; stoves, in the shape of an antique urn, mounted upon pedestals, grates of all kinds, and in the best taste, for coal fires . . . kettles, tea-pots, sauce-pans, frying pans, neatly and solidly tinned, spades; hoes of different sorts for cultivating the sugar-cane . . . bas-reliefs after excellent models for the backs of fireplaces—in a word, everything, down to cast-iron hinges and bolts for doors; and most of these last-mentioned articles are so moderate in price that a man of very limited means may here procure many articles of necessity, and even of ornament, which he could not obtain elsewhere at three times the price. But labour and workmanship are here supplemented by machines and ingenious processes whereby the work is hastened and made more perfect.'

Faujas saw much else, but as he tells us 'I was not at liberty to take notes'. This in fact was quite usual; some years earlier two engineers from Berlin, visiting the factory in Soho which was managed by James Watt, had taken advantage of his absence and had sneaked into the room where the first steam engine, 'Old Bess', was standing and had taken notes; Watt was justifiably furious. At Carron Faujas respected the rules and was forced in consequence to spend part of the night in his hotel room setting down from memory all the points that seemed to him useful to know. The importance of the foundry at Carron was certainly great enough to merit Faujas' interest. In fact, the development of the use of iron in everyday life derived from the enterprise and brilliant

53

initiative of John Wilkinson: his contemporaries summed him up rightly as 'the father of the iron trade'.

EARLY STAGES OF THE IRON AGE

The father of John Wilkinson was Isaac, who gave up farming in Cumberland in order to work in a Lancashire forge for a weekly wage of 12 shillings, the normal rate for a day labourer. Isaac was satisfied with his lot and his employer gradually increased his wages from 12 to 18 shillings: Isaac accepted these rises and asked no more. But when at last his wage reached a guinea he realized that if he was worth so much to his employer, then surely he could earn still more working for himself, so he set up on his own. Deciding that his leather bellows were inadequate, he set himself to constructing an iron pair for his forge. His neighbours were scornful. But when Isaac turned his bellows over to steam all had to agree that he knew what he was doing; thanks to his bellows he was able to make iron chairs, vats for the distilleries and breweries, and iron pipes. His son John was to add still more to his father's range of products.

John Wilkinson was not an inventor in the true sense, but he was a man of strong character, quick to understand the significance and the financial potential of other people's inventions. In 1775 he was the first man to order a steam engine from Boulton and Watt, which he put to a use quite different from pumping water in the mines, for he required the new machine to power the great bellows in his works at Broseley.

He was also one of the first, in 1781, to order a rotary engine for Bradley forge. His interests, however, extended beyond England, to the foundries of Wales and the Cornish mines. In 1777 he built forges at Indret in the Loire, and a year later blast-furnaces for the foundry at Le Creusot. Soon he was digging a canal to carry iron barges for the transport of coal to the foundries. Like other pioneers of the Industrial Revolution—Boulton, Wedgwood, Strutt, Arkwright and others—Wilkinson was a remarkable organizer, but he saw farther and deeper perhaps than any of the others, Wedgwood apart: by 1777 he had persuaded the iron-masters of the Midlands to hold meetings three times a year at which they agreed on prices and conditions of sale.

Contemporary writers used to say that Wilkinson had 'iron madness'; but he was no less enthusiastic about its casting; he replaced old iron water-pipes with cast iron, and in 1788 delivered nearly forty miles of these pipes to supply water to the city of Paris. As early as 1767 he was manufacturing iron nails for use in the mines. And by 1777–79 he was building his first cast-iron bridge at Coalbrookdale. A second bridge was ordered by Thomas Paine to be used in America. But when the author of 'The Rights of Man' and the 'Age of Reason' was obliged to leave England on account of his advanced views, he was also forced to abandon his bridge, whereupon in 1796 its component parts were used to construct a bridge over the river Wear at Sunderland. The span was great enough to allow an ocean-going vessel in full sail to pass under it. Wilkinson had erected a Methodist chapel of iron, and in 1805 he was buried according to his wishes in a coffin of iron, laid beneath an iron monument weighing 20 tons. From 1787 tokens of bronze and silver minted by Wilkinson to compensate for the lack of official coinage were so much in demand that unscrupulous manufacturers endeavoured to counterfeit the die.

Intellectually Wilkinson was a man of advanced views—he came to the help of Priestley when the latter's house was set on fire during the Birmingham riots, which we shall mention later. But besides his strong will he possessed a character so tyrannical that his brother William was compelled to part company with him and to set up on his own account at Indret. In fact the brothers were equally stubborn; when they gave up working together they set themselves to breaking up the machines in their Welsh foundries, using hammers to separate the parts into exact halves.

One of Wilkinson's greatest assets was his immediate understanding of the importance of Watt's improved steam engine. Of all the inventions of the reign, none perhaps was more significant. Not only did it enormously increase the productive strength of industry, but also, by reason of the high returns it gave, the capital involved in financing the equipment of new factories took on added importance. The high cost and complexity of materials which the steam engine introduced into factories called for a new type of industrialist, who could organize production efficiently, and who had access to capital as well. It is here that Matthew Boulton deserves special tribute for so clearly understanding these two essential conditions, which made possible James Watt's revolutionary improvements to the workings of the steam engine.

THE TOYSHOP OF EUROPE

Matthew Boulton was born in Birmingham, a city already highly industrialized, having been since the sixteenth century a town 'full of inhabitants, and resounding with hammers and anvils, for the most part of them smiths'. In the eighteenth century Birmingham was beginning to be recognized for the manufacture of shoe buckles, buttons, metal ornaments and toys; the famous orator, Burke, named it 'the toyshop of Europe'. But at the beginning of the century no manufacturer ever left his workshop or his forge or set off to seek new markets. Instead the ironmongers rode to Birmingham to do business; their money in their saddlebags, and their eyes on the despatch of the purchases they were to make. Despite the limited scope of this small and semi-artisan industry, it was still very profitable. Hutton the Birmingham bookseller, who himself had made a fortune, vowed he had seen more than one man come there on foot and drive away in a carriage. Until 1749 the horse was the only transport available, since there were no communications between Birmingham and London: the road from London to Chester ran more than six miles away at Castle Bromwich, and merchandise intended for London had first to be taken there. In 1747 a coach was put into service to ply between the two cities. The journey took two days, 'if the state of the roads permitted'. In 1767 a stage wagon, more uncomfortable but cheaper than the coach, was put at the disposal of less wealthy travellers. Such transport soon became insufficient for the disposal of the products of an expanding industry. Boulton then embarked on a financial interest in the Grand Trunk and Birmingham Canals, especially the latter, since it was to be dug near his factory and would convey his products to London as well as establishing a link with the coalfields of the North which supplied his fuel.

Matthew Boulton's grandfather, John, came of a clerical family from Northamptonshire. Towards the end of the seventeenth century he had set up in the nearby town of Lichfield, where he had married an heiress with a dowry of 'considerable real estate'. But he ran into financial difficulties, and was obliged to send his son Matthew to Birmingham, where he established himself in a small silver-engraving business, and was soon manufacturing a variety of other goods besides. The Boulton family had found themselves the best possible surroundings for the development of

56

their business. Hutton the bookseller, who had arrived in Birmingham in 1740, described his first impressions of the town: 'I had been among dreamers, but now I saw men awake. Their very step showed alacrity. Every man seemed to know and to prosecute his own affairs.'

FROM SNOW HILL TO SOHO

The first Matthew's son, Matthew in his turn, was born in Birmingham in 1728, where he attended school for a very short period. He managed, however, to give himself a thorough knowledge of Latin, French, drawing and mathematics; but his real pleasure lay in the study of chemistry and engineering. At the age of seventeen he was already engaged in improving methods of manufacture of buttons, watch-chains and steel buckles (the latter were exported in great quantity to France, whence they returned to England to be sold as French products). Boulton claimed he was a toy-maker by trade, but he soon branched out into other activities, including, at a later stage, the minting of coins, by an ever-increasing use of mechanization, without allowing his manufacture of ornamental work in stone, glass, and tortoiseshell, as well as in metal, to dwindle. In a letter addressed to Adam in 1770 he boasted that he possessed almost every machine that could be applied to these arts.

By 1759 the factory at Snow Hill had become too small, and Boulton was obliged to set up a new factory two miles north of Birmingham at Soho, building on a piece of waste land, hitherto a rabbit warren. At Snow Hill the workshops had been small enough to allow the employer overall supervision, but the Soho factory was so large that it was necessary to appoint foremen, or overseers, responsible for enforcing discipline in each section of the factory. The new building, which was completed in 1765 at a cost of nearly £10,000, cost as much again to equip.

BOULTON AND WATT

Boulton took a big step forward when he decided to choose as his partner James Watt: Watt was a manufacturer of scientific instruments for Glasgow University. He had made many improvements upon Newcomen's steam engine, which he had patented in

57

1769. At this stage Watt's machine was nothing more than a steam-pump. But when in 1781 the rotary machine already mentioned was invented, a new era opened up. Until then Boulton and Watt's steam engines had nearly all been destined for use in the mines, especially in the tin and copper mines of Cornwall, and had been constructed to specific contracts whereby the machines were installed at the expense of the owners of the mines, who further undertook to pay an annual royalty amounting to the cost of one-third of the fuel they had saved by using the machine. But it was not very easy accurately to assess this economy, even when Watt invented a calculating machine especially for the purpose. There were endless arguments on the subject, and very often Boulton and Watt were forced to accept payment of a fixed lump sum. This problem of the collection of royalties was even more formidable than had been envisaged, since the construction and setting up of the new machine turned out to be extremely expensive: almost £47,000 for the first model. What is more, during this time Boulton had been forced to mortgage or to sell some of the property he had inherited from his father, or through his wife's dowry.

He had, moreover, been forced to borrow money from friends, and take on another partner, John Fothergill—a lively character who understood foreign markets but who did not possess Boulton's unquenchable optimism, and, therefore, foreseeing the inevitable crash, advised him to file his petition in bankruptcy. Boulton refused to listen to such defeatist counsel, and raised still further loans, notably from a London bank, to allow him to keep going. In this way, between 1768 and 1780, Boulton invested a capital sum amounting to almost £20,000 in research while his accounts for the same period showed a deficit of more than £11,000 net. It was not until 1787 that the business was once more set on its feet as a going concern.

LABOUR

Boulton understood the importance of good relations between staff and management. We have Boswell's anecdote of the workman whose employer had confiscated his furniture: '. . . find you a friend or Neighbour,' Boulton told him, 'who will lay down one half of your rent, and I'll lay down the other half.' But this savoured more of out-of-date paternalism than of any new method. Much more significant was the ceremony he organized in 1791 to celebrate his son's coming-of-age: a procession of workmen divided into grades and led by a band was followed by an enormous banquet for 700 workmen, at which Mr Boulton's health was drunk and likewise the future owner's. In fact Boulton was merely adapting to industry the traditional custom whereby landowners celebrated their sons' coming-of-age. Even the mutual insurance society which he instituted was nothing new—this sort of organization was frequently set up and run by the workers themselves. His real innovation was the rule by which a compulsory deduction was made from wages ($\frac{1}{2}$d on a weekly wage of 2s 6d, and 1d on 5s, 4d on £1, etc.). These subscriptions went into a fund which paid out in case of illness or accident. Boulton encouraged the workers to sign contracts lasting four or five years, whereby a worker's wage would rise from 11s to 15s between 1780 and 1790, and from 15s to 21s between 1790 and 1800.

The expansion of the business led to problems in recruitment; as the need increased, so it became more difficult to find responsible qualified workers. If a skilled workman became overfond of drink Boulton would close his eyes as far as possible to the fact and resist Watt's demands that the culprit be sacked on the spot. Boulton was essentially a realist, and he understood the difficulties of replacing qualified workmen. Moreover one must remember that boxing, cockfighting and drink were more or less the only amusements of the working classes under George III.

THE INDUSTRIALISTS AND INTELLECTUAL LIFE

Boulton spared no efforts to produce ever more precise and powerful machines. He wished, just as Wedgwood did with his pottery, to improve the aesthetic quality of his products. He made vases, bronze ornaments, tripods, etc., and consulted Adam the architect and decorator, and Flaxman the sculptor for the designs he used. In any case no branch of science could ignore Boulton, who corresponded with Benjamin Franklin about steam engines as well as magnetism, electricity, and many other scientific subjects. It was at this date that lively groups of intellectuals rose up or expanded in industrial and commercial towns like Liverpool, Bristol, Newcastle, Norwich, Warrington and Manchester. In 1768, on the occasion of Watt's visit to Birmingham, Boulton invited his friends to *'l'hôtel de l'amitié sur Handsworth Heath'*, as he had named his house, to meet the Scots inventor. These guests formed the small nucleus of the 'Lunar Society'—so called because its meetings were held at the full moon, so that those members living outside Birmingham could return home by moonlight. Artistic and literary, as well as scientific discussions were held at these meetings. Besides Boulton and Watt, members of the Society included Josiah Wedgwood, Thomas Day, the author of *Sandford and Merton*, the printer Baskerville, Sir Joseph Banks, President of the Royal Society, and the astronomer Sir William Herschel. Doctor Erasmus Darwin (grandfather of Charles Darwin), poet, botanist and philosopher as well as Doctor of Medicine, was regarded as patriarch of the Society, while in scientific matters Doctor Priestley took the chair.

DIFFICULTIES AND PERSECUTION

In 1780 Priestley had been appointed minister of the Presbyterian congregation which met in the New Hall in Birmingham. But Priestley had not only communicated to the Society the results of his experiments upon the composition of air, and shared with Boulton his passion for chemistry. He had also found at the Society's meetings an atmosphere favourable to ideas on progress and liberty. Then when the French Revolution broke out he evinced so much sympathy with its cause that the Irish statesman, Burke, denounced him before the House of Commons; and on July 14, 1791, the people of Birmingham, at the instigation of magistrates hostile to new ideas, demolished the chapel in which Priestley ministered and set fire to the philosopher's house. They destroyed his books and his laboratory apparatus, as well as the manuscripts in which he had recorded the results of twenty years' research. During riots which lasted for four days, the house of the bookseller William Hutton was sacked, and so were the non-Conformist chapel at Kingswood and several other buildings. With cries of 'Down with the philosophers!' and 'Long Live the Church and the King' ringing in his ears, Priestley fled to London and from thence to America; Boulton's name headed a fund opened for his benefit, to which John Wilkinson subscribed £500.

The Lunar Society struggled on for a few more years, until it came to an end in the hostile atmosphere of the Napoleonic Wars.

Even so, as late as 1809 Leonard Horner, on a visit to Soho, could write of 'the remnant of the Lunar Society', and the impression made by 'the remarkable men who composed it . . . is not worn out, but shows itself to the second and third generation in a spirit of scientific curiosity and free inquiry which even yet makes some stand against the combined forces of Methodism, Toryism and the love of gain'.

BOULTON'S END

These lines were written in the year of Boulton's death, on August 17, 1809, at the age of eighty-one. The patent on his steam engine had lapsed nine years before. But during that time Boulton had never completely lost interest in the business, in spite of the fact that fifteen years before he died he began to suffer from gout, the disease of this century, and four years after this from stones in the kidney which were to plague him until the end of his life. From time to time he would go to Cheltenham Spa for a cure. But even there he would keep in touch through his partners with the affairs of the business. He demanded laboratory apparatus so that he could make analyses of the Spa waters, recording the results in his notebooks. Thomas Day died in 1789, Wedgwood in 1795, Doctor Withering in 1799, followed in 1802 by Doctor Darwin and by Priestley two years later. But Boulton's passion for work and for science saved him from mourning too deeply the loss of his old colleagues.

CHAPTER TWO

MONEY

In 1776 (the year in which the Soho factory completed the first example of Watt's machine which Wilkinson had ordered), during a conversation with Boswell, Boulton had declared: 'I sell, Sir . . . what all the world desires to have—Power.'

This lust for power was characteristic of most of the new industrialists, and Boulton was no exception. He was prepared to use any and every means, legal ones included, to obtain his power. Jonathan Hornblower, whose machine was more advanced than Watt's and not a mere copy, was prosecuted and ruined by Boulton and Watt for infringing their patent. They complained incessantly about attempts by foreigners to steal their secrets and pass them to Russian, French or German industrialists. But they themselves had developed a similar system of espionage: the German Ebbinghaus had been instructed by them to ferret out the secret of white metal from Saxe-Gotha, while in Paris Solomon Hymen was attempting to steal from the French the secret of ormolu. Bargum, the founder of a Danish company, and Adam Afzelius had been entrusted with similar missions and were endeavouring to entice away foreign workmen for Boulton's benefit.

While Boulton, like the majority of important industrialists of the period, enjoyed his business dealings and the exercise of his authority, at the same time he did not fail to realize that his profession was not universally considered 'respectable'. When, in 1760 he had wanted to marry the daughter of a landowner near Lichfield, her family had objected strongly 'on account of Mr Boulton's occupation'. He overcame this opposition and was accepted. But after such a marriage he would normally have been expected to retire from business altogether. He did no such thing. Indeed, since he was in need of money to expand his business, one of the first assets he sold was the property at Packington which his wife had brought him as her dowry.

Watt, like Boulton, was more interested in the development of industry than in the pursuit of a fashionable life among the aristocracy. When the London mill he had built was ready in 1786 and there was some idea of marking the occasion of its opening with a masked ball for high society he exclaimed: 'Whatever connection has a mill with a masquerade of dukes, noblemen and noblewomen?' Yet this same man built himself a fine house at Heathfield with the money he had acquired from the mill, and laid out a park in the surrounding ten acres of common land—which he had bought and enclosed in the tradition of the noblemen whom he affected so greatly to despise.

Nor was Boulton's life free from little inconsistencies: 'The Empress of Russia,' he wrote with pride, 'is now at my house, and a charming woman she is'; the 'charming woman' sent him her portrait, and it was for long on show in Soho. If Boulton spent much time at the British Museum, reading or drawing, and bought works of art at auction sales, lending them to the Dukes of Northumberland and Richmond for copying, as well as to Lord Shelburne, the Earl of Dartmouth, and the Queen herself, he did not do so from motives of ingenuous snobbery but from a drive to manufacture 'tasteful' products, and so once and for all to obliterate the painful epithet of 'Brummagem', which evoked the nobility's contempt for products from 'the Toyshop of Europe'. The satisfaction with which he talked about the noble lords and ladies who came to visit the factory was unconcealed:

' Last week . . . we had Prince Poniatowski, nephew of the King of Poland, and the French, Danish, Sardinian and Dutch Ambassadors; this week we have had Count Orloff, one of the five celebrated brothers who are such favourites with the Empress of Russia; and only yesterday I had the Viceroy of Ireland, who dined with me. Scarcely a day passes without a visit from some distinguished personages.'

This sort of remark may have proceeded not simply out of innocent vanity, but also from a very understandable desire for publicity. But other more significant aspects of Boulton's behaviour revealed that he did think along the same lines as the 'gentry'. Like all the great landowners, Boulton was convinced that the enclosure of the common lands on which the poor had always pastured their animals was in the best interests of all:

'I founded my manufactory [at Soho] upon one of the most barren commons in England, where there existed but a few miserable huts filled with idle beggarly people, who by the help of the common land and a little thieving made shift to live without working. The scene is now entirely changed. I have employed a thousand men, women and children in my aforesaid manufactory for nearly thirty years past. The Lord of the Manor hath exterminated these very poor cottages, and hundreds of clean comfortable cheerful houses are found erected in their place. Thus the inhabitants of the parish have been trebled without at all increasing the poor levies.'

This is an intriguing statement for it displays the pride of the pioneer, creating employment and well-being for the masses, together with the spirit of the traditional landowner anxious to avoid an increase in his own taxation—with an added touch of the philosophy of the English eighteenth-century middle class, to whom it was mortal sin not to make a contribution to the development of industry and trade—that 'idleness' denounced by Locke, Defoe and Hogarth. If the poor really deserved Boulton's accusation of 'thieving', it was because they cut branches from trees or dug up peat to burn, and picked berries to eat, and rushes for their basket-making—all of which Boulton considered to be stealing, because he tells us, the poor 'have no legal title to the common land'. If in fact 'the captain of industry' did embody a new type of individual, he was clearly one who still had a great deal in common with the great landowner. And yet during the eighteenth century, a vast change came into operation.

Captains of industry, or to use a less precise term current in contemporary writings, the 'manufacturers', existed long before George III came to the throne. But they did not fall into a special class or specific group of people; this is evident from the fact that the word 'manufacturer' at that time could denote, according to context, either a workman or an employer. Around 1720 the English industrialist often sheltered under his roof and shared his board with a number of workmen who laboured with him in his workshop. He was at once master, companion, mechanic and capitalist. Nowadays there is no such class of person, and in his place we are likely, increasingly often, to find capital held by a limited company, only remotely connected with production in the real sense, while the business undertaking itself represents above

3. Heaton House

a. Sheraton chair

b. Chippendale table

c. Chippendale chest
d. Hepplewhite chair

all a complex of share capital at varying quotations and prices, designed to facilitate the conduct of vast financial operations. In fact production tends to become more and more dependent, not upon the needs of the economy but upon speculative business investment. In the course of such changes not only has the eighteenth-century 'master' entirely disappeared, but his contemporary, the 'owner' is also becoming a figure of the past who may eventually find his place in the industrial museum: the 'management', that faceless entity midway between the board of directors and the mass of workers and foremen, cannot truly be said to represent him.

Somewhere between these two extremes of organization methods, the master manufacturer of the seventeenth and eighteenth centuries and the limited company of the twentieth, the reign of George III witnessed the development of the captain of industry. He was a man who was at once proprietor, manager and mechanic —sometimes inventor as well; but he was also a capitalist, although it was becoming increasingly essential for him to choose one or more partners in order to raise sufficient capital. He did not work with his hands, but he gave employment in his factory to hundreds of human beings of every age and of both sexes. If he were to succeed he must possess many and diverse talents, and especially a gift for organization. He was a pioneer, a hero, who inflamed the imagination of his contemporaries. He was a great leader—an 'iron chieftain' as Boswell called Boulton. From this time on, and through three-quarters of the nineteenth century as well, the great industrialist was to be the outstanding personality (as in the twentieth century it is the great financier, the big speculator), distinguished by such salient qualities as courage, determination, optimism and faith in the future.

These wealthy men of George III's reign concentrated their activities in the Midlands or the North of England, while London remained as the centre of the business world with its conduct of commercial and financial transactions.

THE WEALTHY

In the business world, especially in London, everyday life was dominated by the hours at which the Exchange opened and closed: 'They rise rather late and pass an hour at home drinking tea with their families; about ten they go to the coffee-house, where they spend another hour: then they go home or meet people about business: at two o'clock they go to Change, on their return they lounge a little longer at the coffee-house, and then dine about four. . . . Dinner concludes the day, and they give the remainder of it to their friends. . . .' Business could wait till tomorrow! In the winter these friends would meet again at their club, but 'in summer the remainder of the day is passed either at home, walking in the country or in some of the public walks, or in a country excursion if they happen to have a villa near London. About ten at night they go home to bed, after taking a slight repast.' The French traveller describing this day in the life of a businessman between 1765 and 1770 forgot to mention the most widespread evening pastime of all—card-playing—universal in every walk of life.

The household of the rich businessman usually contained a cook, a children's maid, a maid of all work, one or two housemaids, sometimes a groom, and a coachman who was generally hired by the year, and did not live in the house. Towards the end of the reign merchants and businessmen tended on the whole to move out and live in the suburbs of the capital, only setting out for London after breakfast. When a businessman had guests he was quite content to entertain them in an inn or a coffee-house. His wife and daughters had been brought up in boarding schools where they had been instructed in behaviour as well as in the gracious arts: drawing, music, dancing, needlework and French or Italian. The famous Mrs Thrale, whose husband was a brewer, must be regarded as an exceptional case—a bluestocking—she composed Latin verses.

SHOPKEEPERS

The opinions of travellers from abroad were divided as to the behaviour of the shopkeeper in England. Grosley complains bitterly of a case in which a London bookseller was not only clearly negligent in carrying out an important order, but demanded to be paid before the goods had been despatched. Against this a German, Herr Forster, praised the extremely obliging ways of another shopkeeper who offered to deliver a purchase worth 2s to the customer's house, 'although the house was situated at the other end of the town'. It appears that some shopkeepers would offer a glass of wine or a cup of chocolate to the purchaser, or even invite him to dine.

Another Frenchman—M. Pougens—stated just the contrary. But every traveller was agreed on the quality of patience in the English tradesman, who was always good-humoured even when asked to display as many as a hundred bales of material. He was also exceedingly honest, and according to M. Grosley, writing in 1765, there was no haggling as on the Continent: 'You must take it or leave it.' But in fact his supposed rule was far from being universal in the provinces, or indeed in London itself, where in certain quarters it was considered, as we shall see later, a dangerous new custom. The convention of buying outright, M. Grosley tells us, had been borrowed from the Quakers, and was a great convenience to the public: 'A child can do all the shopping as well as a man who knows the current prices exactly.'

What Grosley failed to mention was the solidarity among Quaker tradespeople, as well as generally among members of minority religious groups—the Methodists for example. An instance of this communal loyalty is illustrated by the account of the fortunes of a bookseller, James Lackington, when he first set up in business. In 1791 Lackington published his *Memoirs* with his portrait on the flyleaf, under which is the legend: 'James Lackington, who a few years since began business with five pounds, now sells One Hundred Thousand volumes annually.'

A BUSINESS SUCCEEDS

James Lackington was born in 1746 at Wellington—a small town in Somerset. His father, a cobbler and an alcoholic, first set up in business on his own, failed, and from then on had to work for others. He was soon obliged to stop sending the young James to school, for he could no longer pay the day-boys' fee of 2d a week. The child was able to read but could not write until, in his early twenties, he taught himself. His father, an unreliable workman, as many in this century were, went to work for a fortnight in the county town of Taunton for an Anabaptist cobbler who took an interest in James and turned him into apprentice. But against his master's will he attended Methodist meetings at which one of the preachers was also a former cobbler. There he was converted. Admittedly his faith was to relapse at intervals or perhaps it is truer to say that his conduct did not exactly conform with his principles. Once he was twenty-one, his apprenticeship finished,

67

he went to work in Bristol where he ran into a young cobbler called Jones; and together they agreed to spend their earnings in gay company. But they 'lived hard and worked hard': James listened to the preaching of John Wesley and was once more converted. He longed to educate himself. He would not only read edifying authors, but also a life of Epicurus; whereupon he took to sleeping for just three hours a night, and existed on a diet of bread and tea, both in emulation of the self-discipline of Epicurus, and to save money to buy more books. Around 1768 he was leading the semi-vagrant life of a cobbler's mate in the neighbourhood of Bristol and Exeter. The preaching of George Whitefield, the Methodist minister, strengthened him yet further in the faith. In 1770 he returned to his first love, a dairymaid called Nancy Smith, in the little village near Taunton, and married her: they set up house in furnished lodgings in Bristol, where, after they had paid the rent of 2s 6d a week and bought enough food to last a couple of days, they were left with exactly one halfpenny. James never managed to earn more than 9s and that only in a good week. Nancy learnt to sew ladies' shoes from stuffs—but as an inexperienced worker she made very little money. His friend Jones, now left alone, was furious with James for deserting him and so demanded repayment of a debt of 40s from James, who was unconvinced that he did in fact owe it. It was the last straw. Yet somehow James managed to repay over a period of two months. In spite of a very hard winter which resulted in exceptionally high expenses for lighting and heating, Lackington and his bride managed somehow to exist on about 4s 6d a week; they drank water—never beer or tea—and an occasional cup of coffee, though more often this was replaced by a brew of roasted wheat-grains. Meat was a luxury; if there happened to be any it was invariably made into soup. The Lackingtons were content with their lot; they were faithful Methodists and they loved each other. They were happy and hard-working.

But hardly had James finished repaying his 'debt' when both husband and wife fell ill. Their landlady brought them food, since she did not mean to forego her rent. By this time there was only 2s 9d left, with a further 2s 6d kept under lock and key in case of absolute necessity. Thanks to this provision they were able to subsist for two or three days.

Fortunately James recovered without the aid of medicine or doctor. But Nancy remained bedridden for nearly six months, suffering from violent headaches, which made her groan aloud with pain. Her recovery was retarded by the marked contrast of her earlier life as milkmaid in the country, and her present sedentary existence in the dingy town. For the whole of six months most of James's earnings were spent on medicines for Nancy. He himself lived for the most part upon gruel. Eventually some old woman recommended some 'snuff for the brain', and the pains in Nancy's head at once disappeared. But her general condition still gave cause for anxiety; James would take her back to her native village from time to time, but they could never stay long, for he was forced to earn his living. They spent most of their time in Bristol. The day came when, hoping to find work at a higher wage, James decided to go to London. He was forced to leave Nancy behind with what money he could spare, and in August 1774 he took the coach to London, travelling on the exposed roof, where the seats were uncomfortable but cheaper. After two days' journey he reached London, his entire fortune amounting to 2s 6d in his pocket.

Here he was in luck. The fellowship of the 'gentle craft' of cobbling and the community feeling attached to the Methodist faith were to be his salvation. In fact James possessed something still more valuable than the 2s 6d in his pocket—the address of a cobbler's mate, a Methodist who had achieved his highest ambition by becoming not a freeholder, but the holder of a long lease (very few Londoners owned freehold property). He could no longer afford the upkeep of the house and the rent, and so he let out almost all the rooms. Before another day had gone by this colleague had found him lodging and work as well.

And yet at first sight Lackington does not seem an impressive character, although he had acquired more self-discipline since his marriage. Before it he had had a child by a girl in Taunton, which fortunately for his pocket was still-born. He loathed London: there was more vice here even than in Bristol. The sacred nature of Sunday was certainly even less respected here: people went out, got drunk, fought among themselves as they did on every other day of the week. Lackington wondered how the Lord could suffer such a sink of iniquity, it was clear that the time had come for the last hours of this 'second Sodom'. Fortunately he was soon to discover that in London there were as many followers of Wesley as there were sinners.

Within a month by dint of hard work James had succeeded in

69

saving enough to send for his wife. When she reached London Nancy was helped by a Methodist shoemaker to find work to do at home. Husband and wife were both earning their keep by now, and were able to buy a few clothes. For the first time in his life, James bought himself a woollen overcoat; the shopkeeper wanted 25s for it, but he persuaded him to part with it for 10s 6d; Nancy bought herself a coat as well—in silk.

A short while later Lackington received news of the death of his grandfather—a gentleman farmer in Somerset—who bequeathed him, not the property he had expected, but a mere £10. The executor of the will deemed this too great a sum to risk forwarding to London; so James was forced to travel to Somerset in mid-December, seated on the roof of the coach as before, in order to claim his legacy. But on the return journey so dire was the cold that he took refuge in the luggage basket where he was violently jolted about with cases, parcels, and trunks. When he climbed down on arrival he realized that the money he had had in his pocket—two weeks' wages, 16s—had disappeared. Luckily he had taken the usual precaution of sewing the rest of his fortune into the lining of his coat, since the risk of meeting with highwaymen was always in mind.

With this money James and his wife purchased various household articles but it was too small a sum to furnish their house to any great extent. They had once again to practice 'low living and high thinking' and, by December 24, 1774 they were left with 2s 6d to buy their Christmas dinner. It was unfortunate that James was responsible for the shopping: he set out for market, but on the way he passed a secondhand bookseller where a copy of Young's *Night Thoughts* was displayed. He paid exactly 2s 6d. for the book of poetry and then returned home, the promised meal forgotten. But since Nancy shared her husband's faith, she was soon persuaded of the lasting qualities of the soul in comparison with the transient pleasures of the body.

Some time later Lackington learned from another Methodist that a small shop with living quarters at the back was available to let in the working-class district of Clerkenwell. James was enthusiastic and the Methodist friend set about obtaining the lease. But when Lackington explained that he wished to set up as bookseller rather than cobbler this same follower of Wesley introduced him to other Methodists, who sold him a whole sack of books for only a guinea. These, with his own little library, formed the nucleus of his shop.

Lackington's domestic life was as stern as ever. He and his wife attended every meeting held by the Methodist congregation, to which they belonged as a matter of course, and in addition they listened as often as they could, daily if possible, to the Methodist preachers at the 'Foundery'.

It went without saying that they kept the Sabbath conscientiously; Nancy would not even cook a potato, and small beer was bought the previous day. On Sunday they would listen to a sermon at 5 a.m., followed at 8 by a prayer-meeting; then at 10 a.m. they went back to the 'Foundery' to listen to yet another sermon. In the evening, at 6 o'clock they attended the open general Methodist meeting; at 7 they met at a gathering of the congregation of repentant sinners (see p. 159), and at 8 they joined yet another prayer meeting, after which they made their way home to pray in private.

Lackington's shop was very small and situated in a poor district. Its stock was of little value—perhaps £5 at the outside. But when he looked at the shop-front with his name painted on it he felt happier than Nebuchadnezzar when he cried out 'Is not this great Babylon, that I have built?'

Of course at first things were difficult. But once again the brethren, 'Mr Wesley's people' came to his aid. The Methodists kept an emergency fund out of which they offered loans for three months to brethren in need. So Lackington borrowed £5. Life was as austere as ever of course—the only drink was water, the greatest delicacy potatoes. But within six months the shop's capital value had risen from £5 to £25; whereupon James decided to set up in a small shop near Moorfields, a more central area than before, and here he remained for fourteen years. The premises were larger this time; besides a shop in front and quarters behind, there was also a kitchen and an attic.

But once again James and Nancy fell gravely ill, victims to one of those 'fevers' so widespread in the eighteenth century, and the prevalence of which was not out of keeping with the name of their new district, for Moorfields implied a marshland district. Nancy, who for the past four years had suffered constant ill-health, all the time struggling to keep up her own work, could not survive the extra strain. As an ardent Methodist she had for some time, if her husband is to be believed, renounced all worldly pleasures. She died surrounded by a number of Methodist preachers, and since James himself was ill she was buried without him seeing her again. The nurses who cared for Nancy were constantly drunk on gin, and when they left they stole most of her clothes. Had the shop not been locked up by the Methodist brethren at the start of the Lackingtons' illness everything would have been pillaged. As well as taking care of their possessions these worthies put forward the money to cover their current expenses.

When, by January 1776, Lackington was well again, he remarried. His new wife and former landlady from now on would be there to keep shop whenever he was away. For some time he had reconciled himself to the pleasures of the body and abandoned his faith; when the 'Wesley people' passed his shop he would watch them shake their heads, lift up their hands, and 'turn up the whites of their eyes'. Some of them tried in vain to bring him back to the fold; Lackington was inflexible but justified himself by saying that he had been influenced by the number of hypocrites he had observed among them—dignitaries whose behaviour had not been consistent with their protestations of faith. However it is obvious that in belonging to the movement he had been adequately helped through the critical moments of his life, particularly at the start of his career in London.

By 1778 his business had expanded so satisfactorily that he employed a sleeping partner (current practice in the eighteenth century), which allowed him in 1779 for the first time to publish a catalogue, 12,000 volumes in all. This association lasted for only three years, for it seemed to his partner (an oil merchant) that too much capital had been locked up in books. From the year 1780 Lackington decided he could no longer allow the usual practice of giving credit to customers, and from now on he sold second-hand books at the price marked on each volume. The next edition of his catalogue ran to 30,000 volumes, and in the year 1791 alone Lackington sold 100,000 volumes, realizing a profit which bought him a further 4,000 books. Even supposing that these figures were slightly improved upon for reasons of publicity—a normal custom —it is still obvious that he had 'succeeded'.

Clearly he was no longer obliged to live on bread and water and potatoes. After he had remarried, whenever he spotted a friend in the street, he invited him to share a tankard of good beer. A few years later his invitation included a joint of roast veal followed by, in later years, ham, and still later by a pudding. As with food so the drinks he produced for guests served to mark the different stages of his success—at first a glass of brandy and water was a luxury, but now it was 'Mr Beaufoy's raisin wine', and finally came that drink of persons of quality—a good bottle of ruby port. One more sign of success was Lackington's portrait, painted by a fashionable artist named Keenan, whose portraits and miniatures are still appreciated. It was clearly a very good likeness, since when Lackington's little dog Argus caught sight of it he rushed at it to show it the affection he was used to devoting to the model.

But the apotheosis was not complete until Lackington could buy his country house, at Merton not far from Wimbledon, to the south of London. Here he retired at weekends in his own carriage with his own servants in livery; Lackington's social status was now completely established. Finally to obey both his doctor and the dictates of high fashion he would go to spend a few weeks in a watering-place: at first to Freestone in Lincolnshire—a spa frequented mostly by farmers and tradespeople—and then to Buxton in Derbyshire, where the 'gentry' seemed to think that to ride in any weather and to drink endless bottles of claret could in no way interfere with their health régime. Afterwards he stayed at Lyme Regis on the Dorset coast—then a most fashionable watering-place, a spa whose name alone seemed a guarantee of high tone and a warrant of elegance.

THE 'GRAND TOUR' OF THE MIDDLE CLASSES

While a stay at a watering-place was a mark of distinction, the Grand Tour of Italy and France was an integral part of the aristocratic education. But Lackington had neither the time nor the taste for these cosmopolitan activities. His own Grand Tour would unite education with profitability: he would emulate Defoe the manufacturer and tradesman, and tour his own island; he would visit the least elegant of towns such as Leeds, Preston, Manchester, as well as Carlisle, York, Newcastle, Glasgow and Edinburgh, and so enlarge his market and discover rare and strange books. A prudent businessman, Lackington realized how to combine pleasure with profit, without ever losing sight of the strength and range of his own success.

Success in itself is good, but to appear very successful is even better. And of course the most gratifying experience of all is to demonstrate your success to those who once knew you poor; after all these are the ones best able to realize how far the victor has travelled.

TWENTY YEARS ON

In 1790, therefore, one bright July morning, Lackington set out from his house at Merton, now his main residence, to take the road to Bristol. This time, however, he did not take his seat on the roof of the coach; he travelled in his own carriage adorned with his own crest: 'Small profits do great things.' He wanted to see once more his native town of Wellington, to visit Taunton where he had been apprentice and cobbler's mate. In each of these boroughs the arrival of the great man was hailed by a carillon of bells; and with his brilliant turn-out, escorted by servants, Lackington called upon his old employers. This time there was not a citizen in Taunton or Wellington who did not claim to know him; not a single woman who did not remember having held him in her arms or at some time rocked his cradle; naturally the poor were especially full of such memories—Lackington generously believed them, although at times their lack of years made this difficult. He gave each one a shilling. One and all congratulated him on remembering his humble beginnings, and they begged him to promise that when he was able to retire this son of theirs would once more return to spend his declining years amongst them—the ultimate stage of a highly successful career.

SUCCESS AND ITS REWARDS

It would have been foolish to deny—indeed Lackington had never done so—that Methodism had helped him by the solidarity of the support which he had enjoyed from the outset. But the faith had helped him in a still more important, although indirect way, of which Lackington and his co-religionists were probably quite unaware: the virtues of frugality, temperance, determination and self-restraint, in other words the conditions which ensure success, could only have developed in him by the practice of the Methodist faith. In his *Confessions* (1804), he was to acknowledge the injustice of his attacks against his religious brethren, and towards the end of his days to become an Evangelical preacher (see page 160.

Lackington's success, however, was not entirely due to his religion, but to a lesser extent to the fact that in his way he was a forerunner of modern commercial techniques. To the great astonishment and sometimes great consternation of his contemporaries, he purchased books in huge quantities, not only second-hand, but also the 'remainders' of other booksellers. And since most of his assets (three-quarters of them, he tells us) were devoted to these purchases, he was obliged to sell them quickly in order to ensure a rapid financial return—thus he was forced to content himself with a relatively narrow margin of profit. What is more, every Saturday the weekly budget of receipts and payments was presented to the employees to encourage them to take an interest in the firm's future success. This orginal combination of modern methods of buying and selling with the semi-patriarchal practices Lackington employed, accounted at least in part for his success.

By the time George III ascended the throne the tradition of patronage by the nobility towards writers had come to an end (see page 27). But, in line with the tradition of the past, writers still tended to satirize the successful man of business. Samuel Johnson himself continued to ridicule these men who were so transparently eager to buy country-houses on the pretext that the air in London did not suit them, and who imitated so slavishly the lives of the nobility. For a 'shopkeeper' to aspire to 'grandeur' struck Johnson as ridiculous. To him and to most of his contemporary men of letters the 'parvenu' tradesman was invariably despicable and vulgar, incapable of conversation, devoid of intelligence. As a matter of fact this was often by no means the case. More than one of these rich tradesmen possessed a fine library. The banker William Roscoe studied botany, the fashionable learning of the day, and what is more appeared in the list of the founders of a society in Liverpool designed to encourage painting and sculpture (1773), which organized the first exhibition of painting ever to be held in the provinces. He wrote, too, a biography of Lorenzo de Medici, and another of Pope Leo X. Lackington was happiest of all when he was with friends at home, with whom he could discover some scientific project or other. During these meetings Lackington and his guests would learn to use the microscope, the telescope and the terrestrial and celestial globes, electrical apparatus, pneumatic machines, and an air rifle into the bargain—all the time keeping a good bottle of wine in circulation. This thirst for knowledge, even when it manifests itself—as in this case—in a somewhat naïve manner which may raise a smile, is nonetheless worthy of respect.

PART THREE

LIFE IN LONDON

CHAPTER ONE

A PROSPECT OF THE TOWN

THE OLD AND THE NEW

Every contemporary writer of the time made a distinction between the 'old' London and the 'new' London.

The nucleus of old London was formed by the City with its population of almost 150,000 people: not very large in comparison with the half-million inhabitants in new London when George III came to the throne. A large part of the City had been reconstructed after the Great Fire of 1666, and up to the reign of Queen Victoria it did not alter to any great extent. Right through the reign of George III it remained a labyrinth of little dark alleyways and narrow passages, where many tradespeople lived next door to their shops, their stores, or offices, and where the young Dickens could still watch housewives watering tiny gardens with great care.

But after 1760 the rich tradesmen began to move away to the new districts lying to the west, while in the City public buildings and monuments were gradually rebuilt in a style which, though certainly ponderous, offered nevertheless a standing rebuttal of the charge of Philistinism which aristocratic circles further west had laid, and still continued to lay, against the world of trade and industry. This restoration was largely due to George Dance, the City of London's chief of public works. It was he who cleared London Bridge of its encumbering houses. In 1770–78 he rebuilt the prison at Newgate, turning it into an impressive architectural essay. He also rebuilt St Luke's Hospital, the Church of All Hallows, and gave the Guildhall its new neo-Gothic façade. In 1762 an ordinance was passed prohibiting tradesmen's signs, which on rainy days were wont to shower passers-by, or worse still, in a high wind to crash down upon them, or even, as often happened, to tear down the fronts of the houses to which they were attached, for the shopkeepers had made them bigger and bigger—and consequently heavier and heavier—in order to call attention to themselves.

79

Despite all these changes, the City and its surrounding districts still formed a hotch-potch of buildings, and a vast confusion of alleyways, of courtyards, of passages and nooks. As a contemporary magistrate put it, one had the impression of a great forest in which criminals discovered 'as complete a refuge as the wild beast found in the deserts of Arabia or Africa'. In particular the districts lying immediately to the north of the City, between Smithfield, Holborn and Charterhouse, formed an entire metropolis of malefactors; there were often two, three or four ways out of one house, each giving on to a different alleyway or passage, and the owners of these houses turned a blind eye on their tenants' dubious activities.

The whole of London outside the City, that is to say the adjoining districts of the Strand and Holborn, was ill-designed for traffic. In rainy weather the streets were seas of mud and impassable for pedestrians had they not been intermittently spanned by small hump-backed ways raised slightly above the level of the street—an arrangement which presented obstacles to carriages. In the early years of the reign, streams of water ran down the middle of the streets, when it did not collect in stagnant pools: it was only later, and then very gradually, that gutters were dug on each side of the roadway. In 1765 even the Strand itself was perpetually covered in a 'liquid and stinking' mud more than two inches deep: 'splashing mud, which covered passers-by from head to foot, filling carriages that were without windows and plastering the ground floors of unprotected houses'. And in London itself the streets were more often than not paved with cobbles, laid on the ground without foundations so that when it rained they sank into the earth. Raised pavements of broad, flat flagstones did not make their appearance until near the end of the reign. Until then pedestrians had no protection from passing carriages, except for a line of stakes planted here and there to delineate the part of the highway reserved to them. Even in the smart districts of the new London street paving was very slow in coming about.

When George III at the start of his reign had to go from St James's Palace to Westminster in order to open Parliament, in some streets (King Street was one of these) faggots had to be laid in the path of the royal carriage to enable it to traverse the permanent sea of mud. Even when the way was clear a carriage journey in eighteenth-century London was not an agreeable expedition; the paving stones, according to one traveller from France writing in 1765, were so uneven 'that even the best carriage rolls as badly as the tumbrils of the butcher boys in the streets of Paris. It is the worst jolting machine any mechanic ever devised.' Although this visitor, like all his contemporaries, admired the width and lay-out of the roads in the western district of London, he had to conclude that 'new London is no less entombed in mire than old London'. Efforts had been made, he says, 'to improve the situation with various underground gutters which aim to carry the water from each house to the river, and by digging wells to absorb it, as well as by very strict rules against the throwing of water from the windows'. Despite these arrangements (the one which dealt with the ejection of water or other liquids through windows was completely ignored right up to the beginning of the nineteenth century), and the incessant 'coming and going of great carts to carry away the mud', the best streets in these new districts remained 'in the same state of filth' as those of old London.

Nevertheless there were many aspects of the city which foreigners admired, and of which Londoners could boast: there was Westminster Bridge, for example, which had been completed ten years before George III's accession; but even more impressive was Blackfriars Bridge, begun in 1760 at the outset of the reign and opened to carriages nine years later. This bridge was the work of a Scots architect aged twenty-five who, in the teeth of opposition from all and sundry, including Doctor Johnson, had boldly discarded the conventional semi-circular arch in favour of an ellipse.

Foreigners who unreservedly admired the beauty of both constructions were nevertheless surprised by the height of the parapet of the new bridge at Westminster, which deprived passers-by of the view of the river. This design may have been introduced to discourage attempts at suicide, for which the English were notorious throughout Europe in the eighteenth century. It did not seem likely, however, that the Londoners who strolled over the bridge on summer Sundays had any desire to end their lives: some were there to breathe the purer air, others amused themselves by standing under the arches and blowing hunting horns so that they could listen to the echoes.

To the west and north-west of the nucleus formed by the approaches to Westminster at the beginning of the century, new and elegant quarters were springing up and being extended all the time. Tobias Smollett tells us that in one new quarter 11,000

F

houses were put up between 1763 and 1770; unfortunately he does not specify precisely where. This period of seven years corresponds almost exactly with the period of development which followed upon the signing of the Peace of Paris between France and Spain, only to be checked and slowed down by the American War of Independence. The general effect was very fine: 'I arrived in London towards the close of day,' writes Grosley in 1765. 'Although the sun was still above the horizon, the lamps were already lighted upon Westminster Bridge, and upon the roads and streets that lead to it. These streets are broad, regular and lined with high houses, forming the most beautiful quarter of London.' And yet the new parts of London with their attractive proportions, their fine views and the sober elegance of their buildings could still be criticized for the poor quality and unsoundness of their structure.

For once Londoners and foreigners were in agreement. The same M. Grosley whom we have just cited observed that the walls of houses were clad in a single layer of bricks, 'and these bricks, made from the first earth that comes to hand and barely baked in the fire, are hardly as good as the squares of petrified earth baked by the sun which in certain countries are used in buildings instead of stone'. And a few months earlier the *London Chronicle* of June 2, 1764, had written: 'Let any person attend to the continual accounts given in the papers of the number of half-built houses that tumble down before they can be finished, and he will tremble for those who are to inhabit the many piles of new buildings that are daily rising in this metropolis.' According to this report the trouble arose because 'the demand for bricks has raised the price for brick-earth so greatly that the makers are tempted to mix the slop of the streets, ashes, scavenger's dirt and everything that will make the brick-earth or clay go as far as possible. The scavenger, unwilling to be kind to the landowner, has doubled the price of ashes, trebled the price of cinders, and charges a considerable price for the filth, mud, and what they call the slop of the streets. This slop makes near one-half of the composition that is to raise the enormous and numerous buildings which are to unite London with Highgate, Bromley, Romford, and Brentford within five years.' And the paper concludes: 'The legislature has provided for our safety against the roguery of the builders, but unless the materials of which the bricks are made shall be taken into consideration, London may shortly resemble the city of Lisbon, without the intervention of an earthquake.' These prophecies were exaggerated, and London never bore the slightest resemblance to the ruins of the Portuguese capital after the notorious disaster to which the newspaper refers. But this kind of pessimism was still abroad even half a century later—and there is an echo of it in the following words written by a Londoner in 1808, who was convinced that since the beginning of the century many lives had been lost as a result of defective building: 'I am certain', he wrote, ' that there are today at least three thousand houses in danger of falling, both in London and in Westminster.'

And yet the writer allowed that in 1808 'pure air circulates in the new streets; and the squares are carefully planned, and pleasing to the eye; the upper-class society who live there find these squares salubrious since within each of them is a magnificent garden; the surrounding houses are tall with plenty of big windows . . . admirable pavements very wide protect the passers-by from carriage and carts from which they are separated by an edging of stone raised above a wide stream. . . . The splendid façades of the banks and the insurance companies, many of which are ornamented by beautiful carved emblems above the door, superbly decorate the streets of London. The efforts of our fathers in the improvement of houses and streets leave us scarcely anything more to do.'

The rosy conclusion is almost as extravagant as the *London Chronicle's* forebodings forty-three years earlier. Our informant seems unable to grasp that London in 1808 was lucky enough to enjoy conditions conducive, if only temporarily, to health and the planning of the town. One of the primary effects of the Industrial Revolution had been to remove heavy industry to the coal centres in the North and Midlands of England, leaving London with artisan manufacture and light industry alone, and these tended to leave living conditions in the capital unaltered, whereas towns like Manchester, Liverpool and Birmingham were victims of their own expansion.

Nevertheless, with the exception of the tanneries and breweries, the long-established workshops of London which are described for us by visitors from abroad and which did not affect living conditions in the capital, were almost exclusively factories for luxury goods, and secondary industries or assembly workshops. We can read of a cabinetmaker's workshop in 1786 employing 400 apprentices, carpenters, sculptors, gilders, silverers and carpetweavers,

83

and in which craftsmen worked in conjunction to achieve a single completed article—a chair, sofa, writing-table, secretaire, chest of drawers, dining-table and so on. Nearly every visitor from abroad at some time described the workshop of Hatchett, the saddler and coachbuilder, who employed a team of specially trained workmen to produce carriages and harness. His workshop was 'evidence of the arts and trades brought together, lodged, and established: the coach painter, the sculptor who decorates them, the labourer who manages the workmen: smiths, carpenters, locksmiths, 2,000 workmen work all day in his workshop'. There is a description of a bookseller who, as well as selling books in his shop, controlled a number of workshops situated in various basement rooms where the books were printed, stitched and bound. What strikes the modern reader is the fact that these great London businesses were really large factories, or more precisely a congress of artisan workshops which had little or no adverse effect upon the health and the life of the town.

Such optimistic views of the London scene in 1808 were soon outdated: the capital was shortly to be swept up in its turn into the Industrial Revolution and to lose the qualities which distinguished it from Manchester or Liverpool. Further the writer's views on the spaciousness of the city were misleading, since they applied only to the 'elegant districts', and not to the working districts in the East End. According to a German traveller in 1790: 'especially along the banks of the Thames are old houses, with narrow streets, barely paved. The contrast with the western districts is astonishing.'

GLIMPSES OF LONDON THROUGH THE EYES OF A VISITOR FROM FRANCE

The impressions of a traveller from France arriving in London on a foggy day were naturally unfavourable, because, he tells us, of 'the smoke which, mingling with perpetual fog covers London and entirely encloses it'. The fog was not perhaps literally 'perpetual', but in contrast to towns in France, where the only fuel for domestic use was wood, London, where coal was 'the only combustible in kitchens, in rooms, and even in the halls of grand houses', was a disagreeable surprise. 'This smoke, being loaded with terrestrial particles and rolling in a thick, heavy atmosphere, forms a cloud which envelops London like a mantle; a cloud which the sun pervades but rarely.' Even in spring the Frenchman found

'. . . St James's Park incessantly covered with fogs, smoke and rain, that scarce left a possibility of distinguishing objects at the distance of four steps. . . . When the spring was completely opened, all this park, trees, alleys, benches, grass-plots were still impregnated with a sort of black stuff, formed by the excessive deposits which had been left by the smoke of winter. . . . The vapours, fogs and rains, with which the atmosphere of London is loaded, drag with them in their fall the heaviest particles of the smoke; this forms black rains, and produces all the ill effects that may justly be expected from it, upon the clothes of those who are exposed to it. . . . London swarms with shops of scourers busy in scouring, repairing and refurbishing the clothes that are smoked in this manner: this scouring is perpetual.'

THE STREET SCENE

Visitors remarked not only upon the fog, the smoke, the width of the newer streets, and so on. What also struck them, even in the better districts, was the monotonous appearance of the buildings: 'All the houses are painstakingly alike,' writes one visitor towards the end of the reign; 'when you have seen one, you have seen them all. They are so much alike that it is quite easy to make a mistake and to believe that the house next door to yours is your own, were it not for the fact that every door bears a bold copper plate upon it with the name of the owner and number of the house engraved.' The operation of replacing the signboards by numbers went on for so long—from 1762 in London, and from 1765 in Westminster—that by the end of the reign the whole scheme still seemed newly begun.

'Houses in London have only three stories at most, with never more than three windows in front; they are very flimsily constructed. Windows are rarely shuttered.' This 'uniformity' had begun in 1774 when a law had been passed laying down specific standards for every new house, with special conditions affecting its strength and safety. Londoners, until now accustomed to free enterprise, called it 'the black law'. It must, however, be remembered that this sort of measure helped to endow the London of 1780–1800 with the symmetry, dignity and sober elegance which

85

distinguishes the period. But these streets, so well laid out, with their houses almost invariably of brick (later they were faced with stucco to imitate stone) never ceased to provide the astonished visitor with a variety of surprises.

What, for example, were those splendid pots made of Cornish tin which stood, seemingly abandoned, on the thresholds of the houses? They were intended for the brewers who came to deliver at any hour of the day or night. And when the pots were empty they were thrown out 'to enable the tradesmen's boys to collect them when they are passing through that district. . . . I found some at every step I took. . . .' This is indeed a commentary upon the honesty of a populace which, according to police magistrates—from Fielding to Colquhoun—was allegedly full of pickpockets! Here is a decided conflict of opinion.

This same traveller stopped short at the sound of a reedy voice crying: 'Sweep, sweep!' A child of barely six years old ran barefoot trying as he ran to attract the attention of passers-by. Maybe his parents had sold him to his present employer for a few pounds; it was a lot of money, but the smaller the child, the better its price for this sort of trade. Or he might have been stolen from his parents to sell at what he would fetch—by no means an unusual custom. What a thick layer of soot already encrusted the face and half-naked body of the little sweep: these small boys or even girls, were very rarely, perhaps never, washed. They slept in a cellar upon sacks of soot. They were sometimes forced to climb not merely to sweep the chimney, but if necessary to extinguish a fire, and to crawl through circuitous shafts where they might suffocate with the soot, especially in the bends of the chimney. Should they shirk the climb their master lit a fire under them or pricked the soles of their feet. An employer of child sweeps, David Porter, tried in vain to improve their working conditions which at the end of the reign remained as appalling as ever.

It was an agreeable contrast to see pretty girls in white pinafores with black taffeta bonnets, a yoke about their shoulders hung with cords on each of which dangled buckets sparkling with milk. They were usually employed by a dairyman whose regular customers made up a 'milk-round' in a defined area. The milk came from one of the many dairies on the outskirts of London and had more than probably been diluted by the tradesman *en route* with water drawn from one of the gutters which ran along the streets—unless of course the farm itself had already done the job; one farmer had a pump installed in his cowsheds especially for the purpose. In any case the milk, even if pure, would certainly have been skimmed and its cream churned into butter. This pretty milkmaid, were she not the wife or daughter of some Irish labourer working to increase the slender family income, was probably a pauper child whom the parish had got rid of by placing her as apprentice (for a consideration of about £5), to a milkman—an employment which would not serve to teach this pretty child anything of value, so that when at the age of twenty-one her contract came to an end she would have no hope of finding any reasonably paid employment.

But had the spectator of the above scene been gazing too fixedly at the milkmaid, he might easily have broken his neck; for there were gaping holes in the pavement, often partly hidden. This was because pavements in London had been laid over vaults wherein lay cellars, shops and workshops. 'By means of a paving stone which can be raised, the great quantity of coal required for the house is delivered.' This pavement was fenced off from the house by an iron railing and a three-foot area which linked the cellar with the basement. About one-third of the population of London apparently worked and lived beneath ground level. It was up to pedestrians to avoid these manholes, which were usually left open all day (at night they were supposed to be closed down, but were often carelessly forgotten). In front of a wine and spirits shop the visitor might peer inside one of these manholes to see a flight of steps leading to the cellar down which the brewer's delivery men were engaged in rolling beerbarrels. These might have noticed the passer-by, but would have paid him no more attention than if he had not existed; they had no intention of bothering with anyone or anything that might get in their way. A passer-by from France might have been tempted to recall the efficient manner his countrymen had for dealing with such rabble! But here in a land where they beheaded kings it was wiser to tread warily! So, with all the politeness he could muster, he would have asked permission to go by. He would certainly have received a torrent of abuse by way of reply. He was likely to have spoken perfect English, and if he were sensible would certainly have been dressed in an English style. Should anyone suspect him of being one of those whipper-snappers from France sometimes sent over to sell French silk stuffs that had thrown English workmen out of work, then he would have been elbowed into the mud without more ado. So long, of course, as he did not show his willingness to fight by taking off his coat and shirt, in which case the loungers would have formed a circle around him and ensured that the rules and etiquette of the 'noble art' of boxing were observed. For even a 'Papist' with no money for shoeleather—since in France, as everyone knew, they all wore clogs and lived on onions and thin soup—was entitled to sporting treatment. Most visitors knew better than to reply, however, and apart from a few preliminary insults, would come to no harm. In fact whatever the 'insolent mob' might do, the people of London 'although proud and high-handed, was by nature a kindly people, humane even in its lower orders'. The foreigner knew that in London it is not the porter who must make way for the passer-by, but the latter who must take care not to 'prejudice the free commerce of anyone whatsoever; giving way to a man carrying a china vase, to a woman with a hand cart covered with a white cloth, on which are unripe fruits which she sells at a high price, to be eaten then and there; maybe to a child selling meat unfit for human consumption and bought to feed cats and dogs'—to a child or to a woman, since meat for cats and dogs was often sold by the latter. In any case a Londoner, while respecting working people, had no time for mere strollers; 'idlers' were not very popular with this 'republican' people.

The Englishman in the street was in a perpetual hurry:

'Full of their own affairs, they are always right on time for their appointments. It is unfortunate for anyone who stands in their way; constantly darting forward, they jostle with some force since they are bulky and their movements strong [John Bull is massive, Jacques Bonhomme lean]. I have seen foreigners unused to this behaviour let themselves be tossed and whirled about for some time in the midst of a crowd of pedestrians who had no wish but to get on. Having soon adopted the English custom, I ran through crowded streets, exerting myself to the utmost to keep out of the way of people who were equally careful to avoid me.'

Of course Londoners, always in a hurry, would complain about anyone or anything that might get in their way, and so they grumbled at the enclosure put up on the pavements in front of houses under repair or in process of building, since they not only hindered the traffic but served also as hide-outs for pickpockets.

THE TRAFFIC

Londoners complained especially bitterly of the hold-ups in the traffic. Drivers of private carriages would carelessly park themselves on passageways reserved to pedestrians, and the latter were then forced to cross the road in the mud, instead of walking on the pavements. The driver of a delivery wagon, taking advantage at the earliest opportunity of a refreshing glass of beer, might find a procession of carriages drawn up and patiently waiting behind his wagon when he returned. These bottlenecks infuriated Londoners, who were more demanding in such matters than foreigners, especially the French, who believed that traffic conditions in London flowed with relative ease compared to Paris. The secret lay in certain rules which the English had adopted. A visitor in 1765 describing the busiest part of London could say: 'they take great care to prevent the almost inevitable chaos which could result from the eternal passing and repassing of carriages in the most frequented streets, some of which are exceedingly narrow'. The behaviour of the public contributed greatly to the ease of movement of the traffic; they concentrated all their attention 'on preventing frays which in the midst of the perpetual coming and going of vehicles in the busiest and narrowest of streets, would seem to be inevitable'. Admirable too were the self-discipline and composure of the English drivers: 'When, despite the great care of the coachmen and carmen to avoid them, there arises some confusion, their readiness to turn aside, to go back, to make way for another, and to lend a hand generally in case of need prevents this confusion from degenerating into one of those murderous brawls which so often happen in Paris.' Even at the approaches to the more frequented pleasure-spots such as the Ranelagh Gardens in Chelsea the spontaneous self-discipline of the English driver made police control unnecessary. 'Let us even add to the honour of London coachmen of all classes that I have seen 400 coaches together at Ranelagh, which placed themselves in file, passed each other, and were always ready at the first word, without either guards or directors to keep them in order.' The wide thoroughfares in the newer districts made things much easier: in Oxford Street (at this time Oxford Road, and earlier still Tyburn Road), in 1786 two ranks of carriages generally stood waiting down the centre of the road, while on each side there was space for two lines of carriages, which in no way interferred with the convenience of pedestrians, who were still able to walk six abreast on the pavements. In 1786 Oxford Road was no longer (since 1783) the road to Tyburn (now Marble Arch), which the condemned had to take in procession from Newgate Prison in the City to the gallows. And this thorough-fare, which for so long had been rather shabby and short of shops, had now become a busy and elegant commercial centre, the width of the street creating the right conditions for the large number of customers that pressed towards the luxurious shops.

In 1765 M. Grosley was full of admiration for the shops in the Strand, and the adjoining streets. These, he thought, still provided the most arresting sight in London: 'They have doors of glass, and outside they are ornamented with old architectural features . . . carefully carried out, spotlessly clean, and to judge by the things they sell and by their elegance of arrangement they are a sight with which Paris has nothing to compare.' A crowd of shoppers jostled in the courtyards and passageways of the Strand and Holborn: 'The finest shops are spread round these courtyards and passageways. Here you can see elegant society attracted by the choice of goods; their display, the magnificent windows, with their materials or their delicacies for the table, and their serving-girls, are enough to lure the pedestrian inside, quite apart from the cleanliness and the guarantee of safety to be found there.' It is plain to see that London tradesmen in 1765 were by no means unaware of the publicity value of feminine beauty. . . . But the narrow streets afforded certain difficulties for those shops without glass windows: thus for example, shops selling Indian silk and cotton had their decorative columns and pilasters 'covered entirely with pieces of material, all coated from head to foot by the mud which bespattered them continually'.

In Oxford Road in 1786 Frau Sophie von La Roche, the wife of a Counsellor from Coblenz, described how the goods were displayed '. . . in a way more attractive than in Paris or in any other town', especially the stuffs, which were hung and draped artistically to be shown off to as much advantage as though they already clothed a woman's body; while cotton materials of every colour were exposed for the customers' choice. The drapers' shops were among the most beautiful; an orgy of white for every requirement from swaddling clothes to the final shroud. Shoeshops were crammed with every variety of article; while one customer tried on a pair of shoes, her small daughter rummaged in a shelf in order to find a pair to fit the doll she carried.

The exquisite cleanliness of foodshops seems to have delighted Frau von La Roche; in the butchers' shops appetizing morsels were displayed upon cloths as white as snow, and the great haunches hung from the ceiling were set off by the white cloths below them; ceiling, wall and doors were all immaculate—there was not the smallest trace of blood or dirt anywhere, and on the counters the scales and weights sparkled with polishing. Bread in the bakers' shops was also spread out on white cloths; the customers were served by well-dressed salesmen, and the owner was polite but not obsequious.

But pastry-shops were even more attractive than the bakers, and on this score the Swiss, Henry Meister, clearly shared Frau von La Roche's views. Pastry shops there were in plenty: '. . . at least one every hundred yards', and all so clean and fashionable. The visitor from Zurich goes on to list the many sorts of cakes to be bought: raspberry, redcurrant and gooseberry tarts, gingerbread, cakes full of Corinth raisins, marzipan, jellies and many more. And each morning customers of every age and condition would find their way there, apparently under the impression that there was nothing extraordinary in tasting half a dozen tartlets then and there. In 1788 a traveller from France confirmed the views of the Swiss and the German visitors; this was a young gentleman from Brittany, a M. de Cambry, who declared, 'nothing is more delectable and clean than the pastryshops', and he did not attempt to conceal his obvious pleasure in being 'served by pretty shop-girls'.

LIFE AND DEATH

Apart from material details of this sort, foreigners in London were enchanted with the variety of goods for sale, with the sight of busy streets, the obvious but unobtrusive wealth, the contentment plainly to be read in people's faces, their cheerfulness and everywhere and above all 'this pleasurable feeling', to cite Doctor Thomas Campbell, who paid a visit to London in 1755 and found for himself, as Rowlandson's water colours later confirm, that 'Merrie England' was not yet quite dead.

The streets were not perhaps as clean as they appeared to the eyes of this Irish priest, who naturally compared them to his own in Dublin. The gardens which today stand in the centre of London's most elegant squares were enclosed during the reign of George III so as to prevent the tipping of rubbish and to keep out tramps. It was essential, even at the end of the century, to keep well away from the cemeteries in London; the appalling stench which arose from the communal graves or 'poors' holes' could turn the strongest stomach; these graves were dug deep enough to swallow up seven tiers of coffins (three or four to each tier), and the pits were not covered over before they were completely filled. Until then they remained open to the elements, and from them rose the smell of putrefaction. It is wiser to desert these dismal graveyards and return to healthier ground. Let us now look at London by night.

LONDON—THE CITY OF LIGHT

It is said that a certain German Prince visiting London for the first time was convinced that the British capital had been illuminated in his honour—in fact what he saw was the normal street-lighting here. Without going as far as this, other German visitors were also amazed by London's lights. 'I was astonished at the unusually good lighting of the streets', wrote Pastor Moritz in 1782, 'compared with which Berlin makes a pretty poor show.'

Writing of the same period, Archenholz declared that Oxford Street alone contained a greater number of lamps than the whole of Paris put together. M. de Cambry did not agree: he felt that London was 'shabby' by night. As to Londoners themselves—they complained of the way in which the lamps were trimmed and lit by a 'gang of greasy and ill-smelling individuals' who were liable at any moment to upset their nauseating oil over passers-by, or to burn them with their torches of pitch—with the further risk of accident from a rickety or ill-propped ladder. They also thought that their lampglasses were so opaque that instead of intensifying the light they obscured it. It is true to say that no citizen of London has ever felt indulgence towards his public services, and that there has always been a tendency to cultivate a solid tradition of systematic grumbling.

But either way, efficient or not, the public lighting was amply reinforced by the lanterns before every house and shop, especially along main thoroughfares. London tradespeople well understood how thoroughly the artificial lighting emphasized the beauty of their clocks, their jewels, fans, silks, silver, porcelain and glassware. How long past was the time when Defoe had remarked upon the immoral habit of displaying merchandise in order to attract the customer! At the period under review spirit shops were 'especially mouth-watering': crystal bottles of every shape were lit up from behind to enhance, sometimes prismatically, their different colours. Sweetshops and fruit stalls were equally attractive with displays of grapes, figs and oranges, piled in pyramids; sometimes too there were pineapples, a luxury fruit very seldom found for sale and still in 1786 only at the very high price of 6s each. Naturally shops displaying lamps for sale were some of the brightest of all: every sort and size of lamp, in copper or silver, their brightness intensified by a reflector carefully positioned on the floor, great tin drums for oil glittered like silver, and oils of every kind shone through glass jars; there were pretty little boxes designed to hold wicks. An interested crowd was drawn to every shop. It was not surprising therefore that there were so many people in Oxford Street—as many as there were in all Frankfurt when the Fair was on, wrote Frau von La Roche, and they stayed there until at least eleven o'clock every night.

The contrast of Sundays both by day and night was extraordinary. Between the intervals of religious services, every town-dweller was 'on his doorstep, arms akimbo, waiting for another visit to the Church, or for the end of the day; and no other amusement in sight but that of sadly watching the passers-by'. In summer, as we have already seen, a great crowd, mostly of women and children, strolled up and down over Westminster Bridge—but the Thames watermen did not work that day, and the toll charges into London were doubled or even trebled on Sundays in order to keep pedestrians and travellers away. All shows were shut, dancing forbidden, no instrument might be played nor song sung even in the privacy of home, and to the great surprise of the French, 'the public papers [the newspapers] are suspended'.

LONDON'S COUNTRYSIDE

Pedestrians in London at this time found parks as well as streets to stroll in.

Hyde Park was still completely rural; it was not in the centre of London at all, but to the immediate west of the 'Pillars of Hercules', the inn which owed its prosperity to the wagoners who kept communications open with the West of England. The inn catered for a clientele of soldiers who crowded in after drilling or parading in the park. There might be twenty or so of them sitting on the benches outside. Five or six barbers busied themselves with these customers, shaving them, knotting and powdering their wigs, preparing them no doubt for fresh conquests. Hyde Park was also, of course, a meeting-place for duellists.

In London proper St James's Park was still remarkably rural and untouched—very different from the Tuileries or the grounds of Versailles. A Frenchman describes it in 1765: '... nature appears in all its rustic simplicity: it is a meadow, regularly intersected and watered by canals, and with willows and poplars without any regard to order. On this side, as well as on that towards St James's palace, the grass-plots are covered with cows and deer, where they graze, or chew the cud, some standing, others lying down upon the grass. ... At the gate into Whitehall at noon and evening milk is served, with all the cleanliness peculiar to the English, in little mugs, at the rate of a penny a mug.' On the south bank of the Thames in St George's Fields, still quite rural, passers-by could buy milk, this time in urban style from a heated establishment with the elegant Latin name of 'Lactarium'.

Sometimes it seemed as if the most rural areas were contained within the heart of London: the Haymarket, for example, which is today a district of theatres and smart shops, was then an actual market where hay was bought and sold. The hay was pressed between rectangular planks and transported there in symetrical bales, cleanly cut with a razor, and tied round with rushes. (Frau von La Roche calls these bales 'hay cakes'.) Here too were sold trusses of hay, cut and laid with great care—not a stalk out of place. These were all loaded on to carts painted in brilliant colours; the horses were handsome and well-fed, their masters well-dressed. Frau von La Roche felt she was watching the celebration of a national holiday.

Even more pastoral were the outskirts of London—Kensington, for instance, was at the end of the reign of George III still a mere village *en route* to the west, one and a half miles from the 'Pillars of Hercules', which marked the boundary of the capital in this direction. Brompton, very close to Kensington, was still a hamlet, where animals grazed in meadows interspersed with orchards and market gardens. Paddington, a mile to the north of Tyburn, was a village of 340 houses, with large stretches of open land, almost free of buildings. Around 1790 a few dwellings were erected here and rented for about £7 to £12 a year, but the village still remained more or less surrounded by a belt of grassland and farms. To the east of Tottenham Court Road, in the district which today extends over an area to the north of London University, there were very few houses but numerous and extensive fields interspersed with large ponds where Londoners took part in a variety of sporting activities, of which we shall speak later. To the east, in a bend of the river known as the Isle of Dogs (which is not in fact an island) and on Stepney marsh, lay about two hundred acres inhabited by shepherds and their flocks. This was a region famous for its rich pastures where a solitary farmhouse remained.

It would be by no means correct to assume that the sightseer in the suburbs of London had nothing but gay and pleasing scenes to look upon. Some fields consisted merely of shadowy stretches of land littered with heaps of manure and rubbish. Not far from Tottenham Court Road, in Great Russell Street, where the British Museum already stood, a farm of 500 pigs fouled the air. Even in Westminster, Tothill Fields was a rubbish dump which served to fatten pigs. One contemporary saw this place towards the end of the reign as 'the Champ de Mars of the riff-raff'. This was one of the last districts in London to hold regular bouts of bull-baiting. Over the greater part of its perimeter London was edged by a belt of brick-kilns, where beggars spent their nights, cooking their food in the brick-ovens. A contemporary poet was inspired to these stanzas:

> Where'er around I cast my wand'ring eyes,
> Long burning rows of fetid bricks arise,
> And nauseous dunghills swell in mould'ring heaps,
> While the fat sow beneath their covert sleeps.

I spy no verdant glade, no gushing rill,
No fountain gushing from the rocky hill,
But stagnant pools adorn our dusty plains,
Where half-starv'd cows wash down their meal of grains.

Gillray cartoon showing ladies' dress of the future. 1796

6. Iron foundry at Coalbrookdale

CHAPTER TWO

THE HEART OF LONDON

LONDON, THE 'REPUBLICAN' CITY

The rural character of the capital expressed its image and ideal in the person of the Sovereign himself; a King who became progressively more popular after the first symptoms of his mental trouble appeared in 1788. At first only his enemies referred to him in scorn as 'Farmer George' (see page 39), but the nickname became him, and helped greatly to increase his popularity. And all because George III was a very different kind of king from the French and German monarchs. This was clearly illustrated in his home in St James's, and Frau von La Roche was remarkably precise on the subject. St James's Park, where cattle grazed, was 'nature in the raw', said M. Grosley, 'even the Royal Palace seemed middle class and homely'. But the German visitor with her bourgeois background disagreed: 'I prefer the Park to the Tuileries in Paris, although the buildings there look more splendid, just as all London houses are far inferior to those in Paris; but, as I said before, I like this difference, as most of the well-to-do plebea in houses are witness to the fact that England divides up the spoils of nature more equally, just as if a state with a republican spirit, controlling the power of the monarchy, were to keep its ground territory more level, so that the goddess of Fortune might roll her wheel unhindered into every nook and cranny.' The similes of this visitor may be somewhat obscure, but the idea itself is fairly clear. Frau von La Roche had some inaccurate views on the contrast between rich and poor, but the disparity in London was probably less marked than in other capitals. After all, Buckingham House—the Queen's home—was only a rather modest house—attractive certainly, but ordinary. As for simple citizens, the uniform appearance of their houses was to the foreigners' eye the outward sign of their 'republican spirit'.

There is no doubt that foreigners found numerous signs of this spirit, and especially in the way that the London 'proletariat', unlike the Parisian, rubbed elbows with people of quality. This had astonished Grosley the moment he set foot in England: 'Westminster Bridge and the streets filled with coaches, their broad foot-paths crowded with people, offered such a sight as Paris would present if I were to enter it by the finest streets of the Faubourg St Germain or of the Place Vendôme, supposing those districts of the town to be as much frequented by the common people as by persons of quality'. Other factors seemed to reveal this new republican spirit: in the new streets 'the pavements always gain something in width at the expense of the middle of the street', since in London 'those who walk find they have the advantage in every respect', rather than as elsewhere 'the people of quality'. Besides if there were too many carriages the 'great' did not hesitate to descend from them to continue the journey on foot with the rest of the crowd which filled the pavements: 'This happens every day to eminent people of the State, who on these occasions show the worth of their name and the dignity of their rank.'

Everything in London, from the street lighting to the great clocks on public buildings which saved passers-by the expense of a watch, bore witness to this 'concern for the lower orders'. Furthermore such concern was reciprocated: Grosley was struck by the way in which the English labourer at work was always 'full of care for the public and conscious of his own worth'. Frau von La Roche watched the carpenters who emerged at dinnertime from the naval dockyard at Deptford, their sacks of shavings for firelighting over their shoulders; she admired their proud appearance, their self-confidence and intelligent faces. It must, she felt have been the result of the wonderful English education, conducted in schools where, she was certain, the sons of the people mingled with sons of the nobility. Frau von La Roche was once more under a misapprehension. But she could well imagine how these admirable London workmen returned home to peruse the London newspaper and discuss the welfare of the State, proud of a trade which gave them a chance to serve the nation. . . . The picture is again unrealistic, but everything is relative: Frau von La Roche, like Grosely, like Moritz too, comparing England with the 'feudalism' of the continent, was filled with admiration for the 'republican' spirit abroad in London.

LONDON, THE CLASS-CONSCIOUS CITY

This image of London as a world of 'democracy' and 'egalitarianism' is, if not illusory, at least incomplete. Alongside the comparatively democratic London—democratic at least compared with Paris or Berlin—was a less obvious aspect, as a rule not seen by foreign visitors. No capital in Europe, perhaps, could incorporate such a complex and subtle hierarchy of class structure based on so many varying elements: occupation, district, street, type of house— whether it was owned or merely rented, and which part lived in.

M. Grosley was one of the very few visitors to eighteenth-century England to suspect that the term 'populace' was very much less than straightforward, and that underneath it lay a complex situation. He was careful to set aside the 'rabble'—which was made up of the 'porters, sailors, chairmen, and the day-labourers who work in the streets'—from the 'persons of condition', which comprised tradespeople as well as 'the lower class of merchants who keep shops'. Grosley's classification was still over-simplified. For instance even among the day-labourers themselves, the double differences of occupation and family origins created a hierarchy of their own. Francis Place, a tailor, relates that when his employer took on a poor boy as his new apprentice, the child was immediately 'classed' by his workmates as being of the lowest order, not so much because of his poverty as because of his father's occupation. 'He was a good lad,' says Place, 'by no means so disreputable as I and my companions were; but he was the son of a labouring man and had been apprenticed by the parish of Barking. . . .'

From the top to the bottom rung of the social ladder residence formed an important criterion. At the top such enclaves of the aristocracy as Pall Mall, St James's Square, Cavendish Square and Portman Square conferred upon all who lived there the stamp of supreme elegance. Towards the close of the century the newly rich occupied houses in the neighbourhood of Oxford Street, while wealthy or ambitious tradesmen owned houses in Bloomsbury Square, Queen's Square, or Red Lion Square. The average lawyer lived in chambers in Chancery Lane, Hatton Garden or Bedford Row, and less exalted tradespeople—or the more conservative of them—remained around the Stock Exchange, Bow Bell Street, Sheer Hog or Pudding Lane. A more humble section of the lower middle class dwelt in Fenchurch Street, or Lombard Street and

99

its vicinity. The poor artisans and labourers drifted eastwards to such districts as Wapping, Whitechapel, Mile End, or the south of the Thames, to 'the Borough' as Southwark was known. The husband of Mrs Thrale, a wealthy brewer, was a notable exception, preferring to live in the neighbourhood of his brewery. Finally, round about the Old Kent Road and St Giles's every sort of outcast from society could be seen. Of course these divisions were far from absolute, but they were sufficiently valid in 1792 for the journalist, Francis Grose, to consider them an accurate representation of the period.

These districts were each divided yet again in accordance with another clarifying principle: it was more elegant to live in a 'square' than a 'place', and smarter to live in a 'row' than in a plain 'street'; down the scale from the street in descending order of social rank were three sorts of passageway, more or less narrow; courts, alleys or simply passages. An individual's occupation and address were not the only measure of his place in the social order. No less important was the tenure of his house. Land in London was usually owned by members of the aristocracy and other very wealthy people. Most houses were held on a long lease and reverted to the freeholder of the land when that lease expired. The most important tenant in each house was the 'housekeeper', who contributed to local taxation and 'parish rates'. He in turn rented lodgings, usually furnished, to lodgers who were lower down the scale. These lodgers were themselves subject to class-distinctions: 'room-keepers', were simply lodgers slightly superior to the ordinary lodger, for they sub-let some of their rooms to people of lesser means. As for the housekeeper, although liable for various charges, he could also enjoy certain privileges. In case of need a householder found it easy to get credit, or to raise a loan. The superior rank which a housekeeper enjoyed was remarkable, even when he occupied only a single room in the building. And when he fell into poverty he still benefited from a certain moral standing which was always attached to the position of 'decayed housekeeper'.

A lodger's precedence within the household depended on the situation of the room he occupied. The peak position was held by the occupant on the first floor, after him came the tenant of the second floor, and on equal footing the tenant of the garret and the ground floor. Finally and a long way last was the tenant who lived in the cellar. The lodger in the front rooms of each floor was considered superior to his neighbour in the back room. Garrets were often rented by a hack-writer or a poet, although other professions might occupy them; in 1787 a young chemist, John Elliott, rented a windowless garret with no fireplace, furnished with a single lamp, for two guineas a year.

A cellar could cost about 1s to 1s 6d a week in rent. A whole family might live in it, sometimes, particularly among the London Irish, several families together. Often a cellar would be used by a poor artisan as shop and lodging: he would never enter the house, since he could reach his cellar via the area steps. Cobblers, greengrocers, above all milkmen, lived like this. In Monmouth Street, one of the streets most frequented by pickpockets, nearly every cellar was used for such trades. One of them was occupied in 1786 by a young man who paid £9 a year: 'I am a cobbler,' he said, 'I have neither mother nor father, my shoes when mended hang at the cellar door. . . . I do not know the name of my landlady; she sells dresses and other goods and I pay my rent every Monday. . . .' The size of the rent alone indicates that this was a respectable house. There were, however, 'furnished' lodging-houses provided with straw or palliasses only, which the occupants brought with them. The rent for these was usually about 2d for one person and 3d for a couple. In reality each room often sheltered as many as four or five people. Mrs Farrel, who died in 1765, had amassed a fortune of £6,000 by letting off rooms for twopence, mostly to Irish lodgers.

The poor could not always afford a cellar. Some of them, especially in the outskirts of London, slept in sheds. Street singers, matchsellers, and beggars lived in the same way. In 1760 a certain Margaret King declared when questioned: 'I go out and beg all day long in the streets. . . . I pay 9d a week for a kind of room where there is a kind of bed. . . .' The 'kind of bed' was shared with another woman. One woman accused of theft, Ann Barrington, was living in 1782 in one of these sheds in an alleyway, Star Court in Westminster: 'I live all alone. The door will not shut; it costs 6d a week, and these things (the articles which had led to her conviction) were found under the straw mattress I sleep on.' In 1794 in Clapton one of these sheds sheltered a tenant who was stripped of his belongings by a thief; the latter had slipped in by removing some tiles from the roof.

The stalls or booths, where stallkeepers both lived and worked, were even worse than the sheds. Shoemakers often used them. Some of these booths were exceptionally comfortable; a woman who lived in one of them declared: 'I live in South Street, in St George's Parish where I have a stall; I have a bed, and my own door and window.' It was rare to find any form of heating; it seems that during the hard winter of 1768 a shoemaker died of cold inside his own booth.

For those who, still further down the scale, had neither cellar, shed nor booth to live in, there was the workhouse, where at least the occupants benefited from a form of regular assistance from the parish; these were the 'established' or 'settled' poor. Their lot was slightly more enviable than that of the 'casual poor'—those who received only temporary benefits because they had no permanent domicile within the parish: these the workhouse would take in only for a night or two.

Finally, and at the very bottom of the social ladder, there were many who did not receive even this temporary assistance. These were the 'vagrants', quite outside the law, defined by the Philanthropic Society founded in 1788 as 'links which have fallen off the chain of society, and which, going to decay, injure and obstruct the movements of the whole'.

HOUSES OF THE RICH

There was one aspect of the foreigner's image of 'democratic' London which was not altogether false—at least on the surface: the extraordinary outward shabbiness of the homes of the wealthy. 'Noble' houses were few and far between. M. Grosley, writing in 1765, declares: 'I have in all London seen but four houses which can be compared with the grand hotels of Paris: that of the Earl of Chesterfield, that of the Duke of Bedford, and the houses of the Spanish and French ambassadors; and yet these houses, which are built chiefly of brick, have nothing of the striking lustre which the stone known as *pierre de tonnerre* gives to those in Paris.' It was impossible to explain the contrast between the enormous country mansions of the aristocracy and the meanness of their London houses. The reason usually advanced was an economic one—land was expensive. But this was not the only reason nor even the main one; the English aristocrat retained his London house as a pied-à-terre where he could stay while Parliament was sitting—at the most for a few weeks of the year, but the base of his power was in the country where he had acquired or inherited his family estate, which he was constantly 'improving'. Here was his real home, his *residence*—his London house meant little more than a roof over his head.

The most usual type of London house was the 'terrace-house' (a misnomer, since it did not possess a terrace), many of which still survive. They were separated from the pavement by a railing and an area: under the pavement was a cellar or vault, into which as we have seen there was direct access through a manhole (see page 87). The façade of the house was unbroken by decoration for since the Great Fire of 1666, such ornamentation as it had was flat, and windows did not jut out. The interior lay-out was simple; two or three floors above a basement; each floor containing two rooms—one in front, and one at the back, with a staircase and passageway to the side. If the owner were a man of means there might be a larger number of rooms to each floor; but the basic plan remained the same. The basement held the kitchen, servants' hall, pantry and larder. On the ground floor was a drawing-room, a fore-parlour in front, a back-parlour behind. At the first floor front there was a dining-room—at the back a bedroom, and on the second floor two more bedrooms. The attic or garret was divided into four or five rooms for the servants' use. Where the attic was not large enough, they were put up on a bed in the kitchen 'for a servant or for two maids' as one contemporary writer put it. The Londoner therefore, prepared his meals on one level and ate them on another; he slept on the third floor, and received his guests on another floor. One visitor from France likened the feeling to that of being inside an aviary complete with roosts. Indeed right up to the Victorian era wealthy Londoners lived vertically, while many Parisians in the same circumstances were already living horizontally, according to Sir John Summerson.

Joinery in London houses was of pinewood, imported for cheapness from the Baltic States. Early in the reign the roof was laid with tiles, generally unpolished, sometimes glazed. After 1765–70, when Lord Penrhyn started exploiting his Welsh quarries, slate began to take the place of tiles for roofing material, and by the end of the reign led the field. For walls the traditional material was still brick; the best quality of which was either 'grey' or 'red'. Under George III the 'grey' was not grey at all, but a light yellowish brown which the public preferred; red was no longer used except to frame windows; this was often 'Windsor' brick—bright red and easily tailored. Inside the house partitions were often made of inferior quality bricks or 'place bricks', and as we have already discovered see page 82), these could contain as much cinder or mud as clay.

As the years of the reign went by, however, the more elegant section of society tired of brick, and stucco facings were all the rage. Stucco over brick was used by Adam in Hanover Square in 1776, by Wyatt in Conduit Street and by Nash in Bloomsbury in 1783. But the process was not universally employed until the Regency, which became the great period for stucco. Until then stucco used as it is today was completely unknown; all through the eighteenth century attempts were made to use stucco on houses to simulate stone. Horizontal and vertical lines were drawn to represent free quarry-stone, and each mock-stone was then painted in fresco to imitate the action of the weather on its surface.

Oolithic stone (or limestone) from Bath was the most sought-after for imitation—it was too expensive for any but a few noble residences, but it was easy to copy in *trompe-l'oeil*. Other artificial materials simulating stone were also coming into more general use. Of these Coade stone is the best known; very resistant and therefore useful for outside ornamentation and for the making of columns to support the more magnificent residences.

THE WEALTHY IN LONDON

In London, as in the country, the rich had a way of life all their own. It was quite different from that of lesser men, not just because of the way meals were eaten at a different hour (breakfast was served at about ten in the morning by which time the poorer people had already been at work for the past five or six hours), but also because their pursuits were so different. While the men went out riding, returning in order to go to their clubs, the women read, sewed or played the piano until it was time to go visiting, or shopping. In the early part of the century a lady 'paying a call' did not descend from her carriage: instead she sent a footman to leave a card engraved with her name. When the Stock Exchange closed at 4 p.m. everyone met again for dinner. This was served at five, six or even seven in the evening, but the hour grew later as the end of the reign came in sight, and as the higher scales of the social ladder were attained. Supper was served at an indefinite time—at any hour between 10 at night and 2 in the morning.

Society functions and amusements included morning receptions or levees given by the great, luncheons or dinners to which they invited their guests, card parties, balls, sometimes masked, supper parties and, as the years of the reign declined, 'routs' with up to a hundred or two hundred guests. Dancing took place in a drawing-room marked out in coloured chalk for the figures of the dances; the rooms were illuminated by chandeliers, and by a centrepiece of wax candles. Guests crowded into the supper room while the street outside filled up with carriages. At the end of the century, on Sundays between February and May, ladies drove out in their carriages accompanied by gentlemen mounted on horses, in order to be seen in Hyde Park. In winter they skated over the Serpentine in Hyde Park, or on the canal in St. James's Park. On other days they visited exhibitions of painting, in the evenings the theatre, followed by a visit to one of the pleasure gardens of the capital— Vauxhall, Ranelagh or perhaps the Pantheon.

Once the King's birthday had been celebrated on June 4 'Every-one' left town. They returned to their estates if they owned a coun-try house or a 'place' (that is a castle or a palace). Later in the century they took themselves for a few weeks to one of the fashion-able watering-places: Scarborough, Margate, Ramsgate or Brighton and other resorts. From the beginning of the reign 'Everyone in London' was accustomed to desert the city on Saturday for the country or the suburbs, there to spend Sunday, returning only on Monday in time for the re-opening of Parliament or the Stock Exchange.

THE FINANCES OF A MINOR CIVIL SERVANT

In 1767 John Edwards, bachelor and minor civil servant, was employed in Admiralty, where he received a salary of £50 a year. He lived in Golden Lane, a nondescript street, in a three-storied house in which he occupied a room on the second floor costing just 2s 6d a week. He was lucky to find a room at that price in this sort of street. His bed was topped with a little canopy, and he lay on a mattress filled with a mixture of feathers and flock. He wrote and took his meals at an oak table, but to sit on he had nothing but two old and broken chairs. A small looking-glass framed in red deal hung on the wall. The room was heated by a small iron stove with fireguard, poker, shovel and tongs. An iron candlestick lacquered with copper held the single candle which lit the room. On the table lay an iron pint-pot, a phial for vinegar and a white cup used as a salt-cellar. The room was decorated with a couple of engravings framed in whitewood and unglazed: one was a representation of 'Queen Esther and King Ahasuerus', the other was the famous Hogarth picture 'The Roastbeef of Old England'. This particular household could seldom, alas, afford roast beef! John Edwards breakfasted off bread and cheese, washed down with small beer which he bought for 2d from one of the small grocers' shops known as chandlers' shops, which stocked almost everything. At dinner the *pièce de résistance* consisted of neck of beef, breast of lamb, pig's ear in brine or leg of lamb. This solitary dish was accompanied by a vegetable such as cabbage, potatoes or parsnips, and by a glass of strong beer or porter. The meal cost 7d. Supper was bread and cheese again with radishes, gherkins or onions; this too was washed down with a half-pint of strong beer, and the whole meal came to 4½d. Thus, taking into account the unusually prodigal nature of dinner on Sundays, his food cost him 8s 2½d a week.

John Edward's room was lit by candles; during the cold seasons from Michaelmas Day—September 29—to Lady Day—March 25, he burnt twenty-six bushels of coal at 1s 3d a bushel. Soap, polish, pepper, vinegar and salt were covered by an outlay of 10s per annum. Laundry cost him 10d a week, and twice a week he went to the barber to be shaved and to have his wig combed—6d a time.

His biggest expenditure was on clothes. Although he dressed as simply as possible, he could not manage under £14 a year. His wardrobe held only a single suit of second-class quality cloth (£4 10s), a coat, hat, four shirts of coarse linen, four handkerchiefs, and four of those cravats known as 'stocks', tied loosely at the neck rather like the hunting-stock of today. He never bought anything ready-made; shirts or towels, or stocks or handkerchiefs—he always bought the material and had them made up elsewhere. He possessed a woollen nightcap of course, and in view of the climate and the state of London's streets it is no surprise to learn that he owned four pairs of shoes, which had to be resoled twice a year at the stiff price of 1s 8d.

All in all one has the impression that John Edwards lived less well than many a London journeyman—the 'white-collar worker' is obviously no twentieth-century product! But in contrast to the worker he did enjoy some measure of security.

WORKING-CLASS LIFE

The City, with its banks, its markets, the Stock Exchange, the headquarters of large companies (the East India Company, for example, and the South Seas, Hudson Bay Company and others) was surrounded by four extensive working-class areas: to the north lay Clerkenwell, Shoreditch, Bishopsgate, where numerous artisans especially those engaged in watchmaking and jewellery, lived and worked. Spitalfields lay to the north-east—the haunt of silk weavers: there were brewers, small foundries, forges, naval dockyards, and soap-factories all along the banks of the Thames: finally, on the south bank of the river were the tanneries and the dyers, and a little further up, towards Lambeth, timber yards for building works.

All through the reign of George III the East End (Whitechapel, Poplar, and so on) spread out ever further, but the history of these districts is almost unknown. The great artery of the region was Commercial Road, opened in 1803. For our picture to be true, we must remember that the quarters of the very poor encroached upon the working-class district proper. Eighteenth-century Westminster was riddled with mean little alleyways hardly a stone's throw from the large aristocratic squares. Nearer the end of the reign areas inhabited by the very poor, coincided more or less exactly with those which harboured the constant threat of typhus: the focus of this disease lay to the east of Shadwell, Whitechapel and Bethnal Green; to the north at Shoreditch, Smithfield, and St Giles; the district surrounding Drury Lane and St Clement Danes; and finally to the south, the 'Borough' of Southwark.

These districts, as we have seen, were occupied by workers living in attics, icy cold in winter, poorly lit, draughty and always damp, and occasionally in heavy rain, flooded as well. A working-class family would occupy a single room with one bed sleeping anything from three to eight people, its sheets, if there were any, changed at most three times a year. The room was crammed not only with humanity, and bits and pieces of furniture, but also with the tools and materials required by the father of the family for his trade—

107

and the mother's too, since a great many London workers, including weavers, worked at home. In such a tiny room with so many objects lying about it was impossible to sweep or dust. Broken panes were replaced by pieces of paper; cracks in doors and walls were plugged with rags. And the whole place stank with the excrement from the open drain generally situated at the foot of the staircase.

Even had the wives been able to clean such lodgings, most of them could not have found time, since women of the working class nearly always worked as well as their husbands, and often at the same trade: a shoemaker's wife might, for instance make women's shoes. Others took over jobs which the men did not care to do; the trade in meat, for example, was entirely run by women. Some traded as butchers in the London markets; a day labourer's wife unable to help her husband in his own work would take to selling fish or fruit; Irishwomen incapable of sewing or even of housework hired themselves out as market porters. Many Englishwomen took in washing or sewing. Such employment was essential to them since in most cases a husband's wage was insufficient for the family's needs.

The wages earned by workers at home, notably those of silk-weavers, were usually low. In 1765 rumour had it that one noble lord had declared: 'If I were a weaver at Spitalfields, I would live quite well on 10d a day.' A workman wrote a pamphlet in reply to this extravagance: 'You rot and die every day at Spitalfields, from cold, hunger, filth and vermin.' At this period a labourer could earn from 9s to 12s a week, while a very skilled workman, a typesetter, for instance, might take home a weekly 22s to 27s. The average wage of a journeyman varied from 12s to 15s, but this average rose gradually in the course of the reign: in 1780 to £1, and to 25s in 1795, to reach by 1810 a level of 30s to 35s.

Wages were paid on Saturday nights and always in a tavern, so that, as the magistrate Sir John Fielding wrote in 1761, the workman went home drunk and empty-handed to his family. Generally a workman would be waiting for his pay from six o'clock in the evening onwards, but it was unlikely that the manager or foreman would sit down at the pay table much before 10 or 11 p.m., having as likely as not come to a private arrangement with the tavern keeper. Between midnight and one in the morning the men besieged the pay tables to collect their money, while the women stood guard to prevent their husbands from gambling away the money they had just received. When the workman at last set out for home, often at 3 or 4 a.m. he was drunk and an ideal prey for footpads, who would waylay him and relieve him of what was left of his money. In fact the inn was more than just the establishment in which he was paid. It was an integral part of the life of any working-class man.

DRINK AND THE WORKING CLASS

The public house was often the headquarters of the local organization of a trade, the trade club. This club made its own rules and saw that these were respected in professional matters such as working conditions and more particularly in regard to wages. Each association had its own establishment or house of call, so named because it was the place where workmen in search of a job, and foremen in need of workmen came to call. It was also the headquarters of the benefit society which came to the financial help of members in case of illness or death.

When Henry Nicholson came to London from his native Lincolnshire to seek work as a tailor's assistant, he made his way to the public house which held the headquarters of the trade guild or organization; the trade club of tailors met here, whose secretary kept a register or call-book in which employment vacancies were written down. Nicholson was possessed of a 'document' given him by the local trade club, and this acknowledged him a genuine member of the organization. If there were no work on offer Nicholson had the right to assistance in kind (to bed and board, and certainly to drink), or alternatively to cash. The latter sum was not very great—only 6d in the latter years of the century. A foreman who required a workman might turn up at the trade club at six or nine in the morning, and again at one in the afternoon. Any man he engaged would be taken on in the first instance for one day; if he proved unsuitable he could be sacked when his employer had paid him three hours' work. Had Nicholson been employed even for a single day he would have been liable for a 'footing', or 'maiden garnish', payable to his colleagues according to the trade concerned. This footing, which was exacted from apprentices and new workmen alike, was often very stiff; in the naval dockyard it was as high as two guineas, and anyone refusing to pay was beaten with a hand-saw; hatters were only made to pay 10s. Those who wished to share in this footing were known as joiners, and were obliged to pay a small subscription for drink of 2d. or 3d. But this was only the beginning. Nicholson would also have to pay an assortment of fines under the most varied pretexts such as births, birthdays, marriage anniversaries and the like, not to mention those for any infringement of workshop rules (generally between 1s and 2s). Money raised in this way was of course spent on drinking bouts.

Apprentices had special obligations: one library apprentice was obliged to give a grand supper to the other apprentices, at which he provided two immense bowls of negus and punch. There were initiation rites for youths entering into trade; a London cooper ended his apprenticeship with a payment to his fellows of three gallons of beer; the same obligation of a gallon of beer awaited him for each piece of work he performed for the first time; and an extra gallon for each different sort of timber employed; these special fines were known as 'timber fines'. One cooper's mate was obliged in a single week in 1780 to pay ordinary fines amounting to 16s 4d on top of his footing and timber fines, from his salary of just 15s 9d.

THE SOCIAL ROLE OF THE PUBLIC HOUSE

If one is to see such customs in the proper perspective it must be remembered that the life of every social class at this time in London revolved round the tavern, the ale-house, the public house, and other establishments of the kind. These nearly always contained a parlour for higher class customers, and here the various clubs held their meetings.

Some of these clubs are famous: the Literary Club for instance, to which Doctor Johnson and the painter Reynolds belonged, met every week at the 'Turk's Head' in Soho, and Edmund Burke and Goldsmith were likewise members. Not every club was so distinguished for its literary and artistic figures. The tailor Francis Place tells us that his father, who owned a house where debtors were detained, a sponging-house, belonged to a club which met in the 'Three Herrings Tavern'. This club known as 'The House of Lords', was frequented by barristers, attorneys and clergymen, and well-to-do tradespeople with a taste in common for the 'good life'.

This sort of club was never closed and according to Place no one who had a decent coat to his back was refused entry.

Place's father afterwards kept a public house where several clubs met: one in particular—a punch club—consisted of thirty members who paid about a shilling a night and met every Monday evening at eight, seemingly with the sole purpose of getting drunk between midnight and two in the morning. Two lottery clubs also met there weekly, each member paying a weekly sum towards lottery tickets, and sixpence a head for drink. The cutter club, whose members owned a boat on the Thames, also met in this inn. Altogether thirty clubs held meetings at the 'King's Arms'.

No wonder the visitor from abroad was astonished by the extraordinary variety of clubs. He was unused to the very existence and function of these 'coteries', as contemporary visitors from France called them. There were medical clubs, debating clubs, or spouting clubs where young apprentices practised public speaking. There were chair clubs, so-called because one of the members took the chair at gatherings which were often disorderly. Young people of both sexes could meet at 'cock and hen clubs' to drink, sing and generally have a good time. There were also clubs for bull-baiting with dogs.

A goldsmith–silversmith called Brasbridge, who set up shop in 1770, seems to have led a fairly typical life. 'I divided my time,' he says, 'between the tavern-clubs, the card party, the hunt, the fight, and left my shop to be looked after by others whilst I decided on the respective merits of Humphries and Mendoza, Johnson and Big Ben' (well-known boxers of the time). He enumerates the various clubs to which he belonged, all highly respectable ones: the Highflyer Club, called after Highflyer Hall owned by Tattersall the famous horse dealer whose meetings were, appropriately, held at the 'Turf' coffee-house. He belonged to a card-club which met in Chancery Lane, and to another at the 'Queen's Arms', where he paid a subscription of 6d a week. He was a member of the 'Cider Cellar', famous for its political debates, and of the 'Free and Easy' whose headquarters, also at the 'Queen's Arms' consisted of some thousand members. He also belonged to the 'Spread Eagle' in the Strand, frequented by young men after the theatre: here the landlord once remarked that his were unusual customers since 'what with hangings, drownings, and sudden deaths [he had] a change every six months'.

THE BAD APPRENTICE

Not every employer was like a Mrs Brownrigg, who tortured her apprentices to such a scandalous extent that in 1767 she was hanged for it. But some of the more unscrupulous did do all in their power to render the life of the apprentice intolerable, to drive him to run away and so enable the employer to pocket the expenses attendant on each new contract of apprenticeship—a practice well-known amongst the greedy or the very poor. Others, and they were probably in the majority, without making efforts consciously to profit financially yet subjected the apprentice to such constraints that even if these were common form, sometimes escape seemed to be the only way out for him. In theory he had the right to appeal to the City Chamberlain, but in fact even when a leader or popular agitator like John Wilkes held that position it was very rare for the Chamberlain to attach blame to an employer.

When William Green, a barber's apprentice, complained that his employer refused to allow him out on Sundays before 2 p.m., even when he had finished work, Wilkes admonished him, and reminded him that he had no right to go out without leave from his employer. When William Tomkins, a silversmith's apprentice, complained that his employer beat him constantly and forced him to work on Sundays until eleven o'clock at night, both employer and apprentice were sent packing by Wilkes after a homily. A chandler complained about two apprentices who refused to perform urgent work on Sunday, with the result that both apprentices were sent to prison for three days.

The limits imposed on the freedom of boys, whose apprenticeships had to be endured for seven years, that is in most cases until they reached their majority, must have seemed to them intolerable. And even where an apprentice was treated reasonably well, the temptation to run away was still strong. As a fugitive he might spend the night in one of the brick-kilns or in the covered market, or a derelict house—or if he had any money at all in a night-cellar or low-class lodgings. When he ran out of money gangs of young men would persuade him to go out stealing; and if he later tried to break away from the gang, accomplices would set on him and by blackmailing and generally intimidating him would force him to stay on.

Indeed every circumstance conspired to encourage the young

7. The Bank, 1781

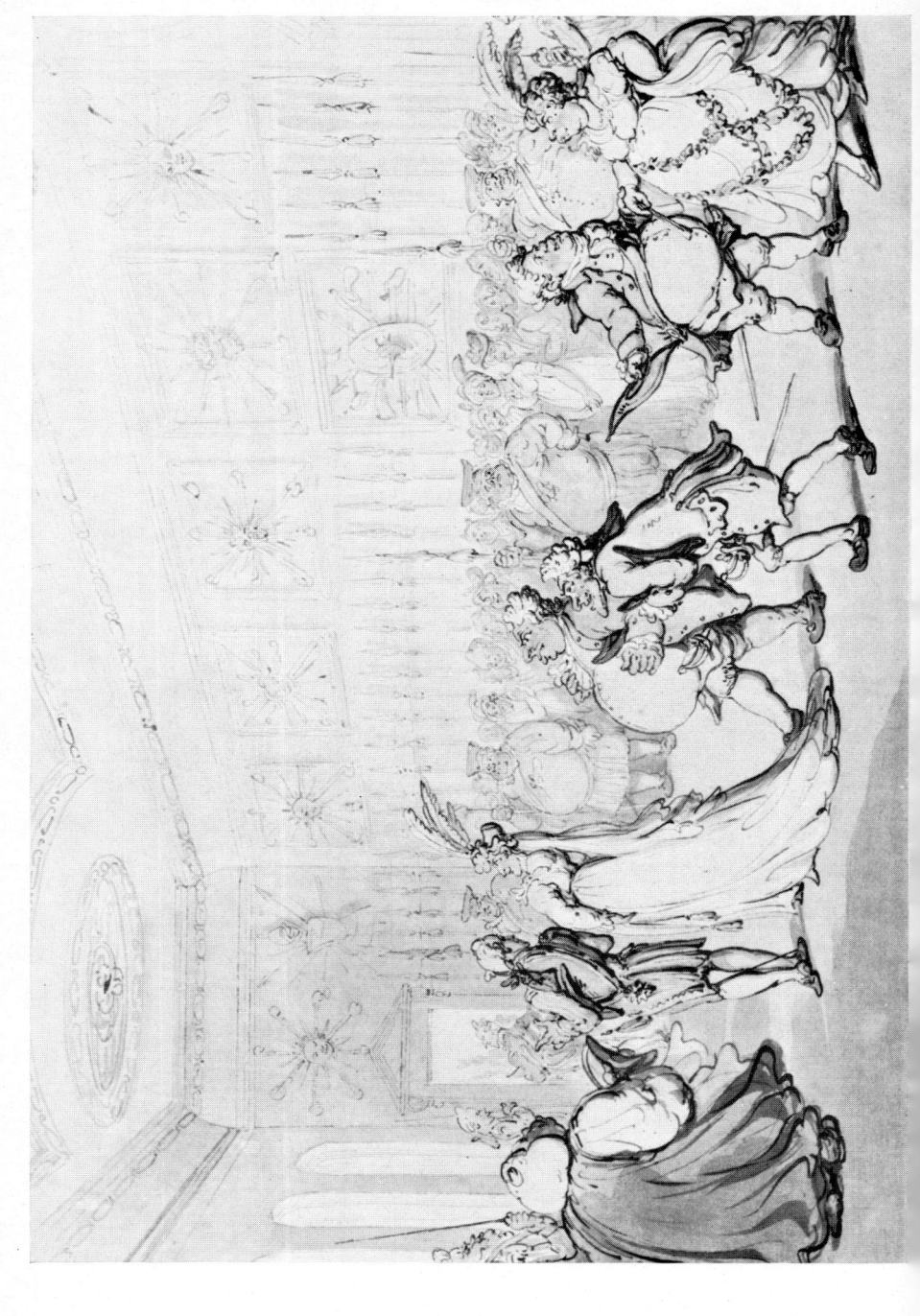

to steal. Shopkeepers were constantly on to children and servants to find out if they had anything to sell: the small grocer or chandler, the fruiterer or greengrocer was often a receiver as well. Young prostitutes whom the apprentices frequented were by no means respectful of private property. Lillo's play *The London Apprentice* is the story of a youth encouraged by a prostitute to rob and kill his master; and this was only a melodramatic version of an ancient tradition dating at least as far back as the fourteenth century; Chaucer's apprentice had the same relationship with a loose woman, who led him into vice and crime.

THE TWO FACES OF THE POPULACE IN LONDON

Work

While an apprentice was subjected to severe restraint during his seven years' servitude this was no indication that he would at once fall into idleness when he regained his freedom. The London workman started work at five or six in the morning, he breakfasted at eight, and dined between midnight and 1 a.m. Usually the day ended at 6 p.m., but many boys, especially in the summer, went on working until eight or nine in the evening. Some ate their midday meal of bread and cheese or bread and salt meat at work, in the workshop or building yard: others lunched at home; many bought a plateful of hot meat and pease-pudding from a nearby cookshop. The evening meal at home often consisted of bread and cheese and tea, which as the century went on came to replace beer. During working hours labourers subscribed to the purchase of beer, and sometimes it was supplied by the employer. When two workmen met in the street their usual form of greeting was likely to be 'What will you drink?' or 'Let's have a glass!'

The above applies of course to workmen engaged in outdoor occupations or in workshops. Tradesmen observed rather different hours, the small tradesman opening his shop at about 8 a.m. and keeping on to a fairly late hour. In 1786 the draper's shop which employed Robert Owen never shut before 10 or 10.30 in the evening, after which everything had to be tidied up, which could keep the assistants busy until 2 a.m. Tailors worked from 6 a.m. to 7 or 8 p.m.; a bookbinder might put in fifteen hours' work daily (up

H

to 1785 when working hours were reduced). The naval dockyards in 1780 were working from 5 a.m. to 8 p.m.

Of course there was no limit to the time spent in work at home. Women's working hours could hardly have been more variable and unspecified. Women who went out to people's houses to do the washing usually began work at about 1 a.m. Ann Nichols, who was washerwoman at the house of a mastermason, would arrive at midnight. In 1765 one woman who went to an attorney's household to do the washing declared that she arrived before nightfall in order to fill the coppers and the washtubs.

Leisure

One must bear in mind the burden of these long hours if one wishes to understand how it was that the rare 'Saint Monday' weekends were frequently extended into Tuesday. The year contained only three official holidays apart from Sundays—Good Friday, Whit Sunday and Christmas Day, added to which were the eight execution or hanging days. According to Robert Southey, the poet, this dearth of holidays (in such striking contrast with the situation in Catholic countries, with their numerous feast-days and holidays), caused working people to squander their few moments of leisure. What is more the opening of theatres in working-class districts always aroused the keenest opposition from the authorities and the middle classes, who feared that the results of an evening spent watching a play might have a bad effect on tomorrow's work. Also, since the law forbade music-making or dancing on Sundays, there was really nothing left for the labourer by way of relaxation. He could drink in a club or elsewhere, join in the games of skill or chance—darts, dominoes, draughts or cards, and so on, which were always in progress in the public houses or taverns, and any money so gained would be spent on drink.

A workman could spend his evening in tea-gardens where other drinks besides tea were sold. A few would make their way to the outskirts of London with their dogs to hunt for duck on a pond; this was a favourite sport of weavers' mates, and a special type of spaniel was bred for the purpose. Others would chase a maddened bull—bull-hanking—through the streets of Bethnal Green: this kind of amusement went on every day of the week, but especially on Sunday, Monday and Tuesday, and anything up to two thousand people would take part: adults or children joined in the pursuit, abandoning their weaving and risking being gored or tossed. Among the watching crowd were the pickpockets, ever present on these occasions.

Sometimes younger labourers and apprentices would club together to buy a boat, in which on free days they rowed up river to Kew or Richmond, there to spend a few shillings in the pleasure gardens. Others, not rich enough to buy a boat of their own, would hire one from Godfrey, the London boatman. It was quite usual on Sundays to see fifty or more boats rowing upstream.

But what else could one do, particularly on weekday evenings, if there were no meeting of the club? There was not always enough money to spend on drink or women. So young men found their way to Temple Bar, the great gate separating Westminster from the City, and from here gangs of them would proceed into the heart of the City, shouting and sweeping aside anyone in their path. Every young man knew how to box, so that if a passer-by refused to move, then two or three of them would fall on him and beat him up. Hooliganism is not uniquely a feature of the twentieth century.

THE LONDON WORKMAN

It is inevitable that the history of this reign, written by members of a ruling class, should dismiss the English workman with the customary epithets of idle, dissolute, profligate, drunkard, and many foreigners took this verdict at its face value and dismissed the working class in the same summary way. Some of these critics even improved upon such assertions, extending them to cover the entire race. Thus in 1777 Lacombe could write: 'The people of England are by nature lazy, drunken and brutal. . . .' The temptation to snipe at the 'hereditary enemy' is so strong and so universal through the centuries that we are no longer surprised. The elegant architecture and furniture of the eighteenth century must not blind us to the harsh facts, and we should never forget how difficult, insecure and precarious a workman's life could be: he was never sure of the morrow; a sudden rise in the price of bread could force him into the ranks of beggars and social outcasts.

Of the twenty-one apprentices whom Francis Place had known only one, he tells us ever became 'respectable', and he had married his employer's daughter, at the same time converting himself to Methodism and preaching its religion. He came near to being the

115

'good' apprentice of Hogarth. But all the other twenty in one way or another had 'gone wrong'. Place and his friends were all members of one of the boating clubs which we mentioned earlier. They were perfectly ordinary young men, neither better nor worse than anyone else; but most of them stole or 'scrounged' to make a little money. The coxswain of the boat was a printer's apprentice and was deported for stealing. The stroke was hanged for a murder he had not committed; although he had an alibi it was disallowed since at the time of the murder he had been taking part in a robbery with some other mates; not that this would have helped, for robbery too was punishable by death. Those who did not get caught up in the law ended their days in the workhouse classed as 'vagrants'.

On the other hand when apprentices did survive in this world where it was so easy to disappear without trace, they became the sort of workmen Grosley praised so highly for their 'respectful attention' towards the public, and also for their industry. M. Grosley was no fool. He understood that it was need alone that compelled them to submit:

'. . . mechanics of the lowest sort, even journeymen themselves, carry English independence still farther: nothing but want of money can compel them to work. If they are obliged to do business they, as it were, fight with their task: they go to it like madmen, and like people enraged at being constrained to labour. They choose rather to toil in this manner, with all their might, and to rest themselves from time to time, than to pass the whole day gently and easily in their employ. The business is carried on the better for this ardour of the artificer; this is evident from the perfection of all English manufacturers, whether of steel or needlework. The tailor in his shop, the shoemaker, etc., is either at work or rests himself: he is seldom keen to trifle away his time in singing or whistling.'

And Grosley bows to the 'perfection of handicraft-work . . . in the lowest class of artificers'.

In reality this 'lowest class of artificers' was not at the absolute base of the social order. Below it again and always ready if opportunity arose, to swallow it up, yawned an abyss of misery of a depth to us unimaginable but which occasionally becomes clear when we read one of those 'anecdotes' from the *London Magazine* which loose an echo from the depths of wretchedness.

In 1763 a prospective buyer was being shown over some empty houses in Stonecutter Street by an agent from Fleet Market who let lodgings. In one of these, on the first floor, the visitors stumbled over the body of a naked woman—the agent ran from the room appalled, while the buyer walked up to the second floor where the agent rejoined him. Here they discovered the bodies of two more women, almost naked. Finally, in the garret were two more women, both still living, and a girl of about sixteen. All three seemed on the verge of starvation. The visitors informed the police, who promptly threw the survivors into prison under suspicion of having caused the deaths of the other three women.

One of the corpses had been Elizabeth Stanton, who had come from Westminster in search of shelter and finding the empty house, had fallen asleep on the ground-floor. Later in the evening at about eleven o'clock the woman Elizabeth Pattent, who had been found in a better state than the others, had come into the room and in the dark had tripped over the woman Stanton, crying 'Who's there?' Stanton woke suddenly and replied: 'Don't be afraid. I'll leave in the morning.' Pattent then invited her to sleep in the garret and together they spent the next two nights there. Elizabeth Pattent had lost her job as a servant and was working as a porter in Fleet Market. Here she met the two dead women who were both known only as 'Bet'. They had taken Pattent to the empty house where they lodged, half-starving, for some time.

During the day Pattent went out to work for her former mistress, who kept a cookshop in Westminster, and was given food in lieu of wages, returning to the house each night. Towards the end of the week before they were discovered, her companions had fallen ill. On Saturday November 12 Pattent pawned her apron for sixpence and managed to buy some beef and a plum pudding in a cookshop in Shoe Lane. On the Saturday and Sunday both women ate well, but on Sunday night they were both taken ill again, one with ague, the other with one of those 'fevers' which we mentioned earlier (see page 71). Pattent, afraid of contracting their illnesses, did not return to see them, and was in prison when she learnt of their deaths.

The girl, Elizabeth Surman, was the daughter of a jeweller off Coleman Street. Her parents had died when she was six, and a neighbour, Mrs Jones, who took charge of her, had died four years later. Elizabeth was found in the street, and told she could get work in Spitalfields, where she was hired as a windster or silk-winder; but her employer retired to the country and the child was once more left destitute. She was again hired as windster to a Mrs Bennet, but was discharged at the end of a week. A Mrs Roach, who took in washing and looked after children, hired her next, and Elizabeth worked there for six years, but was discharged when she became ill. She appealed to the churchwarden of the parish where her father had been for many years a respected housekeeper, to obtain help for her from the local authorities. This sort of assistance was only granted to those legally domiciled within the parish, and the churchwarden refused even to discuss her right to domicile or settlement; he took pains not to let her guess that she had gained, through her years of domestic service, 'servitude' in the parish where she had worked—and therefore possessed a legal right to settlement; he shut the door in her face and, exhausted, Elizabeth spent the night on the threshold where she fell. In the morning the churchwarden, still obdurate, chased her away.

She had slept in the streets until she was told about the empty house, where she lived for almost two months. Later she had lain down next to the two corpses on the straw; she had fallen ill and had eaten nothing. Elizabeth Pattent came to her aid, and when she was better she spent the days begging, and at night she gave Pattent the money she had earned for food. She managed to gain entry to the workhouse of St Andrews in Holborn, but after a week was discharged. Returning to the empty house, she went to live in the garret, and at the time when she was apprehended she had not been out for a fortnight.

Pattent was of course accused of having taken the clothes off the bodies of the dead women in order to sell them; but she denied it, and the charge could not be proved. The coroner was satisfied that the bodies held no trace of violence and that these women appeared to have died of starvation. The jury gave some supper to the survivors and recommended them for a temporary stay at the workhouse. History does not relate what happened next—the whole episode was simply an 'anecdote'.

PART FOUR

LOVE AND LIFE

CHAPTER ONE

IN BROAD DAYLIGHT

Visitors from the Continent, and especially the French, were astonished by the segregation of the sexes in George III's England. M. Grosley did not trouble to conceal his surprise when he came across these gatherings of both sexes:

'All appearances of intimacy between the two sexes is dropped in public, at those meals where persons belonging to different families meet: the women retire soon after the cloth is taken away; the wine is then put upon the table, and the guests begin to enter upon conversation. The ladies accompany the mistress of the house to her apartment, where they enter into a chit-chat by themselves. At the grand assemblies play is the only thing that unites both sexes. If they meet only to chat and converse the women, generally speaking, place themselves near the door, and leave the upper end of the apartment, and all the conversation, to the men.'

Yet despite this apparent segregation men and women formed liaisons of every sort, transitory ones as well as the more lasting, legitimate as well as clandestine. In these conditions it seems extraordinary that any relations between the sexes could take place at all.

LOVE IN THE OPEN AIR

If travellers' tales are true, then it seems that the English of both sexes were prepared to meet and give expression to their affections without the shelter of a roof:

'Bushes and the darkest places, the most remote places in the park, crossing-places and the fields are meeting-places for the secret undertakings of young ladies of high degree; but the daughters of the populace do not seek remote spots for their pleasures, since they have less time to spare; the parish cemetery is the favoured spot for their nightly appointments. More than one girl as a result of her free ways has in her turn become a mother on the tomb of her own parent'.

So, also in the words of M. le Maréchal de Camp, Pillet: 'The cemeteries in England have become places of prostitution.' Maybe the image is too dramatic, the antithesis too perfect to be completely factual. But certainly the London parks were used for assignations, perhaps not by 'young ladies of high degree', but at least by couples who found it dangerous or too expensive to seek the shelter of a room. St James's, the royal park, served the same purpose here as the other parks in London.

Thus Boswell, in 1763: 'At night I strolled in the Park and took the first whore I met, whom I without many words copulated with free from danger, being safely sheathed. She was ugly and lean and her breath smelt of spirits. I never asked her name.' Boswell returned to the park the following week; this time with a large jovial girl; and a few days later he took a girl into an alleyway, where he admits he 'wanted vigour'—which was not very surprising in view of the fact that these encounters took place in March and April, two months which in England are not usually renowned for their warmth. One feels inclined rather, to admire his intrepidity. Bold he could be in other ways as well: when a girl to whom he had given 6d attempted to evade him he did not hesitate to push her by force against a wall. Nevertheless she succeeded in struggling free, and Boswell had to content himself with some forceful oaths. . . . On another occasion he picked up a girl at the bottom of Haymarket, 'and taking her under the arm I conducted her to Westminster Bridge and there in armour complete did I engage her upon this noble edifice. The whim of doing it there with the Thames rolling below us amused me much.' Not everyone shared his taste for such an unconventional setting. St James's Park seems to have been more suited to this sort of amusement: a few months before on these very lawns at Christmas in 1762, the young Hickey (then 13½) went through his first experience of such matters, and in somewhat humiliating circumstances; not only did his own endeavour fail, but the grass on which his campaign was conducted, transferred itself to the knees of his trousers, and the green marks did not escape the vigilant eye of a family friend, which seems to indicate that this use of the park was fairly commonplace.

DIFFICULTIES IN THE PATH OF LOVE

When prostitutes were in question a room could be easily hired by anyone who had the money to pay for it, but when it came to the conduct of amorous activities with a girl from a higher social level the difficulties could be great. According to the Swiss traveller Henry Meister, the obstacles were most acute when the intrigue was in its early stages. A girl of good family, he tells us, would

'. . . make her appointments at some other house either on her return from a walk, from the play, or from a ball. . . . In this country . . . none but the most abandoned women are suspected of intrigue and gallantry. The greatest difficulty is not always to persuade an English woman to suffer you to carry her off, but to find a convenient opportunity for telling her you wish to do it. Amiable and modest as they are, there is less art and good fortune required to bring the love adventure to a successful conclusion, than there is to open it.'

Clearly Meister was referring to ladies of quality in particular, who were chaperoned by servants, not to mention their own families. But ladies of more modest station could also have their problems. Thus Boswell and Mrs Lewis, an actress at Covent Garden, experienced a certain difficulty in attaining a finale which both heartily desired. Mrs Lewis was certainly of sufficient age and independence, nevertheless she was in terror of her landlady, just as Boswell himself was frightened of his landlord: if he happened to return late at night he went in fear and trembling of his reproaches next morning. This same landlord actually threatened his tenant with prison when he suspected him (wrongly as it turned out) of being shut in his room with the maidservant.

When Boswell invited the beautiful Louisa to reply to his most pressing question 'How then can I be happy? What time? Do tell me', the actress replied: 'Why, Sir, on Sunday afternoon my land-lady . . . goes to church; so you may come here a little after three.' Unfortunately for him when the day came Boswell was 'not inspired by Venus'. He made light of the matter and at a later stage was having more success when he heard the landlady coming upstairs. There was nothing for it after this but for Boswell to make his way to Covent Garden, where a service was taking place in the church at between five and six o'clock. Fortunately another Sunday was to prove more successful.

Of course Louisa and Boswell could have taken a room in an inn; they did think of it at one stage. But it meant posing as husband and wife, and in the comparatively small number of inns of a reasonable standard available there was always the risk of being recognized. Besides, it would have been expensive—whereas, as things were, when Boswell had grown tired of the liaison, he was able to record with some satisfaction that he had conducted the whole affair 'with prudence', and had expended a total sum of 18s. In other ways, however, the affair was to cost him more than dear.

'MANLY' DISEASES

Indeed, Boswell soon became aware that he had received a call from the 'Signor Gonorrhoea'—an allusion to the belief that every venereal trouble originated from Italy. On the exact nature of the infection Boswell was naturally rather vague. At first he thought it was merely a mild infection, but as the symptoms grew more severe he was quite certain that he was suffering from a 'distemper' at the very least. He thought of applying to a quack who could cure him quickly and cheaply. But suppose the cure were incomplete? Boswell had reason to be anxious, for this was the third time he had fallen victim to the results of excessive lovemaking; his first disease had lasted ten weeks, and the second four. This time, in 1763, he was forced to keep to his room for five weeks, taking various medicines, and submitting to the 'relief' of several bleedings, for all of which he paid five guineas. In 1776 these 'reliefs' were to be replaced by 'electuaries' and injections; a treatment which cost Boswell only four guineas—two at the outset of the treatment and two when the cure was complete. In between these two attacks, however, during the years between 1766–68, he suffered various mishaps of the same nature, some in Edinburgh and some in London. In 1769 his doctor—a Scotsman—was in a position to effect a cure, but he was prepared to advise Boswell if he so wished to go to London where he might try out 'Keyser's pills'—a remedy now widely-known, thanks to the publicity it had enjoyed in the press. In the end Boswell was to consult Doctor Kennedy, a quack who possessed, nevertheless, some qualifications, since he was a member of the Royal Society. On his advice Boswell dosed himself with the famous concoction Kennedy himself had invented, known as the 'Lisbon Diet Drink', which produced 'a benign salivation', and which could be bought for a half-guinea the pint bottle 'at Mr Woodcocke, the perfumer in Orange Street', if we are to believe advertisements of the period. This sort of publicity, with which the papers were filled, leads us to think that Boswell's case was unexceptional, and that the incidence of venereal disease was frequent despite the preventatives available; the oil recommended by the physician Sir John Pringle, or the simple 'armour' in which Boswell put his faith, and which was acknowledged in a line of verse by the Reverend Kennet (son of the Bishop of Peterborough):

> Happy the Man who in his Pocket keeps
> Whether with Green or Scarlet Ribbon bounds,
> A well made C. . . . (=Condom)

Men of course were not the only victims, and such so-called 'manly' diseases did not spare the women who had been their companions, whether for an hour, a month or longer. Hickey's Nancy Harris, of whom we shall speak later, died of this sort of disease when she was barely twenty-five.

'SENTIMENTAL EDUCATION'

The sexual initiation of boys and girls was, on the whole, left very much to chance, perhaps even more than it is today. It is foolish to generalize on this sort of matter. Yet it does seem as if, at least among the upper classes, the influence of the domestic servant, at this time so numerous, had a definite significance. Domestic servants were often doubtless responsible for those premature sexual initiations. Obviously since there is little written evidence it is difficult to confirm that this was so—very few men were bold enough to confide memories of the sort, even to their private journal. Lord Byron himself held back from divulging 'some secret or other to paralyse posterity'.

But at a guess one can see that among such 'secrets' were the descriptions of his first sexual experiment, a little before 1799 when he was not yet eleven years old, with his Scotch nurse, May Gray; this was how he had 'anticipated life'. When he grew up Byron saw these precocious experiences, doubtless with reason, as a contributory cause of his mental imbalance; but he believed his own experience to be exceptional—he was wrong. Initiations of this kind were not so unusual; but fortunately nor did they always inflict such deep and long-lasting wounds.

Young Nancy Harris, mentioned in earlier pages, was a servant in the household of the Duchess of Manchester, and had been dismissed for having seduced the Duchess's only son, then thirteen years of age. She had been sent away of course, with eulogistic references which enabled her to find other employment, this time with the London lawyer William Hickey. William, one of Hickey's sons, owed his first sexual experiences to this girl. When the lights in the house had been put out she took the child into her bed. One of William's early memories were of a morning when he awoke to find himself between Nancy's legs: 'with one of my hands upon the seat of Love where I have no doubt she had placed it'. William was then only ten years old. This sort of highly incomplete experiment was enough to make him desirous of more perfect endeavours of the kind. The first of these, as we have already seen, took place in St James's Park when he was thirteen, but it proved unsatisfactory; a little later the second attempt took place completely successfully.

Under the arcades in Covent Garden William encountered a pretty girl of fourteen or fifteen at the most. She took him by the arm and offered to initiate him: 'I'll take your maidenhead'. He accepted and followed her into a narrow passage giving on to Drury Lane. And there on the third floor in a shabby room he experienced for the first time the pleasures of life during 'three truly happy hours', and this despite the unforeseen which led Hickey to notice that his chemise was soaked in blood—it appears that lovemaking in this century took place while both man and woman retained their chemises; most of the erotic engravings of the time show men and women in the throes of love with their shifts ruffled. The girl suggested to William that she should go and wash his shirt in the courtyard, while he returned to bed. When she came upstairs again William, who had a half-sovereign in his pocket, generously offered it to her: she refused, however, saying, 'If that is all you have I will not touch it'. Finally she agreed to accept 5s, and, Hickey tells us, she did not own 6d at the time. They were to see each other again often, and each time she would refer to him tenderly as 'my dear little maidenhead'. Hickey remembered her with affection. This reminds one of Stendhal's

126

assertions fifty years later, when he spoke affectionately of the 'kindliness' of London prostitutes: it would seem as if, except in exceptional cases, one of which we shall examine later, there was a kind of tradition about their behaviour.

When he was sixteen Hickey went as boarder to a small private school in Surrey, owned by a respectable widow and run by an ecclesiastic, the Reverend Jackson. Hickey dallied with all the maidservants here, and one of them very often came to share his bed. A few months later when he was taken away from the school after these escapades he found Nancy Harris again and visited her several times, but by now his initiation into sexual experience was complete.

LOVE IN THE ENGLISH STYLE

It is easy to understand, once we have read the *Memoirs* of William Hickey, the reasoning behind John Wesley's question: 'Where is male chastity to be found? Among the nobility, among the gentry, among the tradesmen, or among the common people of England? How few can lay any claim to it at all? How few desire so much as the reputation of it! How numerous are they now even among such as are accounted men of honour and probity who are as fed horses, every one neighing after his neighbour's wife.' Not all 'neighed' after their neighbour's wife, but many of them did not deprive themselves of a young 'filly' to supplement their legitimate companions. The gentleman of high rank whom Hickey met was no exception, although he was well past sixty, married to an accomplished woman who had given him eight children, and the picture of conjugal felicity—a rare feat in the higher spheres of society. He was also the 'serious friend' of Hickey's own mistress. Perhaps we should conclude like M. Grosley that love was regarded

'. . . . throughout the dominions of the King of Great Britain as the most serious of all concerns. . . . The English themselves make a jest of the solemn seriousness which characterizes their courtship. I saw them crowding to a printseller's in Cheapside to purchase two prints of three different colours. They represented a lover and his mistress, both yawning in a manner so natural that the sight of them caused the same convulsion in the beholders.

There are very few personal accounts in this reign relating to the English conduct of the preliminaries of their courtships and relations with women who were not prostitutes. . . . When Boswell was courting Louisa his seriousness and dedication to the conduct of the love affair and its eventual happy conclusion is astonishing. Here is the scene in his own words:

> ' "Madam, I have been thinking seriously."
> ' "Well Sir, I hope you are of my way of thinking."
> ' "I hope, Madam, you are of mine. I have considered this matter most seriously. The week is now elapsed, and I hope you will not be so cruel as to keep me in misery."
> '(I then began to take some liberties)
> ' "Nay, Sir—now—but do consider—"
> ' "Ah, Madam! Nay, but you are an encroaching creature!" (Upon this I advanced to the greatest freedom by a sweet elevation of the charming petticoat.)
> ' "Good Heaven, Sir!"
> ' "Madam, I cannot help it. I adore you. Do you like me?" (She answered me with a warm kiss, and pressing me to her bosom, sighed, "Oh, Mr Boswell".)
> ' "But, my dear Madam! Permit me, I beseech you."
> ' "Lord, Sir, the people may come in."
> ' "How then can I be happy? What time? Do tell me."

We know the rest. This earnestness in the midst of pleasure is perhaps characteristic; but in any case these love affairs even when they were limited to mere embraces and kissing had some disadvantages to masculine clothing: women used such quantities of pomade and powder for their wigs and hairdressing that William Hickey tells us every time he made love to the Charlotte who was to become the great love of his life, it cost him a suit of clothing.

CHAPTER TWO

HALF-LIGHT AND THE DEMI-MONDE

THE GREAT COURTESANS

The gay world possessed a hierarchy all its own, no less than the more serious one. At the summit of this were the 'queens' of the demi-monde, whose favours were sought assiduously as a point of honour by the elder sons of the great families. Next to a university education and on the same level as the Grand Tour such activity was thought to finish off a truly aristocratic education. Towards the end of George II's reign the 'throne' of the demi-monde had been occupied by Fanny Murray. She was succeeded as royal mistress after George III's accession by Kitty Fischer, the daughter of a German tailor, who reigned supreme between 1758 and 1763. Reynolds painted her portrait many times. In 1766 she settled down to marriage with a country gentleman John Norris, and devoted the later years of her life to good works. It was the end of an epoch. From 1760—or thereabouts—the aristocracy moved into a period of relative virtuousness! For some years it was good form to keep an official mistress and to go around with her. The reign of the queens of the demi-monde was succeeded until about 1770 by a period when 'serious liaisons' were the fashion.

'SERIOUS' LIAISONS

There are many examples of this sort of lasting love-affair; the Earl of Sandwich and Martha Ray is one: Lord Seaforth and Harriet Powell, the Earl of Egremont and Mademoiselle Duthé. In some cases the protector would even finish by marrying his mistress. We have already spoken of the marriage of John Norris to Kitty Fischer; and there were many more: thus, the Earl of Coventry married Mary Gunning, the most beautiful woman at Court, whose sister, Elizabeth Gunning, in turn became the wife of the Duke of Hamilton. Viscount Maynard and Nancy Parsons,

I

the daughter of a Bond Street tailor, were another pair. It was a period of relative respectability.

Liaisons of the kind did not always end in marriage. But even without it the exclusiveness of the serious arrangement entitled it to general recognition. Thus when on April 16, 1768 Augustus Henry, Duke of Grafton and First Lord of the Treasury, went to the opera for a gala performance attended by the Royal Family, Nancy Parsons, who was known to have been his mistress for the past four years, took her seat in his box, and after the performance left on the arm of the Duke. This attachment came to an end in 1769 when the Duke was divorced to marry Elizabeth Wrottesley, daughter of the Dean of Worcester. After this desertion Nancy Parsons attached herself to John Frederick, third Duke of Dorset; seven years later she married Charles, second Viscount Maynard. Between 1784 and 1786 she was engaged in finishing the education of the charming young Francis, fifth Duke of Bedford, and it was thanks to this friendship that she was able to shore up her husband's financial position. From 1792 onwards she lived almost exclusively on the Continent, in Naples, Switzerland and France, having finally separated from her husband who was keeping a dancer from the Paris Opera—a Madame Derville. Nancy then retired to the outskirts of Paris where she spent her declining years in good works and where she died, greatly revered by the village people and the priest of the parish.

There seems to have been a certain feeling of democracy among those in high society who formed liaisons of this sort in the first ten years of the reign.

THE RETURN OF THE GREAT COURTESAN

Between 1768–70 the history of the English love-affair seems to have declined somewhat. The day of Kitty Fischer and the queens of the demi-monde returned once more to fashion. It was the ambition of every demi-mondaine from 1780 on to engage the eye of the Prince of Wales, whose gaiety was now reviving the world of pleasure and amusement. In the newspapers and periodicals of the time the names of the highest in the land and those of numerous demi-mondaines are indistinctly printed. Until 1790 there was a 'grand century of conjugal infidelity' with the courtesan as queen. After 1790 the French Revolution and its consequences gave pause to the activities of the English ruling class, and a feeling prevailed that if the tiresomenesses the French aristocracy had endured were to be avoided it might be more prudent to employ some discretion; respectability, at least on the surface, must prevail.

Earlier than this, for some years after 1770, the demi-monde had been dominated by Kitty Kennedy. She was a young Irishwoman whose father was a clerk-usher and among whose admirers were Frederick, Earl of Carlisle, James, Earl of Fife, Henry, Viscount Palmerston, Henry, Earl of Suffolk, Lord Robert Spencer (brother to the Duke of Marlborough), and John St John (brother to Viscount Bolingbroke). She died of consumption in 1781 at the age of thirty-five. But the most astonishing career of all seems to have been that of Grace Dalrymple Eliot.

'TALL DALLY'

Grace Dalrymple was the daughter of an Edinburgh lawyer. Brought up in a convent in Flanders, in 1771 she married a Doctor Eliot, and then formed a liaison with Arthur Annesley, Viscount Valentia, a fine-looking man with some weaknesses of character. After her divorce she became the mistress of Lord Cholmondeley, a good man of extraordinary physique, hence his nickname of 'Mylord Athlete'. In 1779 she broke with him and set out for France where she caught the eye of the Comte d'Artois, brother to Louis XVI. When he left her she replaced him with the Duc de Chartres, son of the Duc d'Orléans. On her return to London she became mistress to the Prince of Wales, and in 1782 she gave birth to a daughter who was registered at her baptism as 'the daughter of His Royal Highness George Prince of Wales'. He neither confirmed nor denied this, and the child was brought up by Lord Cholmondeley, who from time to time returned to Grace. In 1786 the Duc de Chartres, now Duc d'Orléans, offered her permanent residence in Paris, and there she remained throughout the Revolution, while the Duc became first of all 'Philippe Égalité', and in the end was guillotined. Grace did not return to England until 1798. Her declining years are more or less obscure; she was a remarkable woman, even if we cannot wholly accept the part she is alleged to have played in the French Revolution; she must surely have possessed a great fund of courage and intelligence to remain in Paris throughout this time and, despite her liaisons with the

131

aristocracy, to survive. In her hey-day in London she was one of the first of the demi-mondaines to occupy her own box at Covent Garden. Her portrait by Gainsborough was exhibited in 1778. Her unusual height accounted for the nickname 'Tall Dally'.

THE DEMI-MONDE

Kitty Fischer, Kitty Kennedy and Grace Dalrymple Eliot were the 'queens' of the demi-monde, but between 1770–90 it was a demi-monde full of large numbers of beautiful women, often of extreme quality and brilliance. Some of these 'kept women' are well known to us—Fanny Temple, (later to become Fanny Hartford was one of these) of whom Hickey wrote:

'. . . a finer woman in every respect could not be. . . . Her manners were perfectly correct, nor did I ever once hear a vulgarism or coarse expression pass her lips. She was mistress of music, had an enchanting voice, which she managed with the utmost skill, danced elegantly and spoke French *assez bien*. She inhabited an excellent house in Queen Anne Street, and had besides neat lodgings in the country, pleasantly situated near the waterside just above Hammersmith, and kept her own chariot, with a suitable establishment of servants.'

Hickey had know many of these women; Pris Vincent, Newton, Sally Hudston and others. Agnes Townshend did not possess such an elegant turn of speech as Fanny, but she was famous for the phaeton and four-in-hand she used to drive with great dash, and which was known as a *vis-à-vis*, whereby she herself was nicknamed 'Vis-à-vis Townshend'. Another well-known female driver was Kitty Frederick, who was kept by Lord Marsh, better known as Lord Queensberry. There were many other 'town celebrities' among them Clara Hayward, Mrs Sturges, Mrs Latour and Lucy Wells.

One of the most beautiful of all was undoubtedly Emily Warren, the daughter of a blind beggar. Her astonishing beauty caught the eye of an experienced London dowager who adopted her. Sir Joshua Reynolds, attracted by her physical perfection, painted innumerable portraits of her. She died prematurely in 1782 on board ship in the Indian Ocean, in company with her friend Robert Pott, and was buried in Calcutta. Finally there are the two beautiful girls, not over-virtuous, who represented the height of fashion in 1782. They were known as 'Duchess of Portland', and 'Duchess of Devonshire' for they so much resembled these ladies. It was an extraordinary period when authentic dukes married women of humbler birth, while authentic prostitutes rivalled Duchesses in elegance and distinction.

CHAPTER THREE

OUT OF SIGHT

PROSTITUTION

If we are to take M. Grosley's word for it, 'the women of the town' in London were 'more numerous than at Paris and have more liberty and effrontery than at Rome itself'. In 1803 the magistrate Colquhoun put their total at 50,000; others thought the figure to be nearer 70,000. Moralists were naturally outraged. Social conditions themselves were partly to blame, since there was no remunerative light work for women. Added to which there is always a type of man to whom prostitutes are attractive. There is no other explanation for the behaviour of Charles James Fox, the leader of the Opposition who, sought after by a host of beautiful women, still had no compunction in appearing in public (according to Doctor Campbell in 1775) with 'a *putain* of vulgar appearance, a whore more mean-looking than a 2s 6d one on the Strand'. Why else did Hickey, who had the entrée to the houses of the most beautiful women in London (without having to part with a shilling), often prefer, he tells us, to go to 'a bagnio with the most hackneyed and common woman, who not only ran away with my money, but injured my health'. There was, he goes on,

'. . . an extravagant and common little harlot, named Brent, to whom I was strongly attached. She was not at all pretty, being much pitted with smallpox, mercenary in the highest degree, and addicted to drinking. Yet notwithstanding all these failings, there was something about her which fascinated me; and often did I prefer taking her to Malby's, under the piazza of Covent Garden, and there passing the night at considerable expense, to partaking, as I might have done gratis, every species of elegance and luxury at the accomplished Fanny Temple's, or others I have alluded to.'

This 'natural perverseness of disposition' which led Hickey to seek out prostitutes of the lowest order was more common than is generally believed.

134

These prostitutes often attempted to conceal their real business under some fiction as to their true origin. Nanny Smith, whom Boswell took to a remote house in Chelsea in 1776, pretended she was maidservant to a Mr Williams of New Bond Street, who, she told him, had sent her out shopping. But two days later he found her again in a notorious alleyway in Westminster, this time dressed up in a drummer's coat, and she confessed she had been living there for the past three months. This sort of deceit was commonplace. Grosley's assertion that vicars' daughters 'furnished' most of the 'houses' and streets in London should not be taken too literally. Another traveller from France shared his view that most of these prostitutes were 'daughters of the clergy, who had been orphaned and reduced to indigence'. It is clear that a girl of good family who was unable to cope with heavy manual labour had little alternative if she was forced to earn her living. She could choose between prostitution or teaching—that is of course if she had the money to open an academy for girls. This predicament gives some reality to the statements of the Frenchmen. Yet we must not forget that Charlotte Hayes, one of the most famous of London brothel-keepers, did her best to pass off her boarders as hatmakers' or clergymen's daughters, aware that this put up the price to some of her clients; the girl of superior breeding had, as a prostitute, a special appeal to some. When Boswell met a young woman in the Strand who pretended to have been born in Gibraltar the daughter of an officer, he could not resist the pleasures she offered him, and seemed to find them especially delightful on this occasion: 'I could not resist indulging myself with the enjoyment of her.'

BAWDY HOUSES

In houses maintained for prostitution Grosley tells us 'prices are fixed, and all passes with as much order and decency as can be expected in commerce of this nature'. According to another visitor, in the taverns, or rather 'those chop-houses where they also provide for lodgings and for drinking and which conduct a fourth trade, viler but more profitable, they rob you with trickery and swindling'. And, continues this observer, if you followed a prostitute home you risked 'an encounter with some swaggerer or other, and some supposed husband, who accuse you of seducing their wives and who strip you of your belongings and throw you into the street without your shirt, where, far from complaining, the people welcome you with their booing'.

It is not fair to generalize. Of course many prostitutes were dishonest, as were their 'friends', but on the other hand we have read elsewhere of the touching display of unselfishness on the part of the little prostitute who deflowered William Hickey—and there was Kitty Brookes, of whom Boswell remarked, and we can trust the voice of experience, that he had never met a girl more expert at her work. Not only did she not protest when Boswell repaid her with a mere four shillings, but, when he was about to leave and changed his mind, renewing his advances, she demanded no further payment. Boswell the Scotsman was moved by her generosity, and kneeling kissed her hand, praising her virtuousness and vowing that for a 'little' he would have married her!

Prostitutes were to be found in almost every street and in the theatre: Sadler's Wells, Drury Lane, Covent Garden, as well as in haunts of amusement such as the masked balls at the Pantheon, at the Rotunda in Ranelagh Gardens in Chelsea, in Vauxhall Gardens, and on the banks of the Thames: 'At nightfall,' writes Grosley, 'they range themselves in a file on the foot-paths of all the great streets, in companies of five or six, most of them dressed very genteely'. Another visitor confirms this: 'They flood the foot-paths; passers-by have difficulty in avoiding being importuned.' They accosted passers-by, sometimes urging them to 'Come and have a drink', sometimes catching them by the sleeve or tapping them on the shoulder. Then, if persuaded, the passer-by would be taken into 'one of those shops where they sell beer', and which 'serve as their shelter and their workshop. These shops have a room behind and a bedroom reserved for this sort of purpose.' But if the weather were fine then there was always Whitehall Gardens, St James's Park, or even some dark corner of the street. However it was more usual to accompany a prostitute to her room, which was on occasions clean but was more likely to be in a condition of filth.

There were plenty of bawdy-houses, especially in the Strand and in the purlieus of Drury Lane. The 'Rose' tavern, where Hogarth painted his scenes of debauchery depicted in the series 'The Rake's Progress', had been the scene of many strange duels at the beginning of the century, but apart from this was neither worse nor better than many others of its kind. The 'Shakespeare's Head' was much the same. Boswell booked a room there for a few hours and 'solaced my existence' with two young girls 'one after the other according to their seniority'. To the contemporary eye these establishments were not 'disorderly houses' in the real sense.

DISORDERLY HOUSES

However the three taverns near Covent Garden described by Hickey in 1770 richly deserve the title. It is interesting that all three were situated in Bow Street under the nose, so to speak, of the London magistrate, whose offices were in the same street. Sir John Fielding had lost his sight, but, as Hickey remarked, he would have had to have been deaf as well not to realize what went on in his street. It does not say much for the efficiency of the London police force in this reign.

In Little Russell Street the establishments were no better. Let us follow William Hickey and his friends into one of these—Wetherby's—situated in the narrowest part of the street. As they raised the door-knocker of a forbidding-looking door with iron spikes a small barred opening revealed a sinister face which demanded in fierce and raucous tones: 'Who goes there?' To the reply of 'friends' they were permitted to enter one at a time; and hardly had the last one stepped over the threshold than the great door was banged shut; the doorkeeper turned an enormous key in a gigantic lock, slid an immense bolt, and clamped it with a chain. Inside an extraordinary scene met their eyes: men and women perched on chairs tables or benches, were watching a bitter fight between two women; their clothes in tatters, their breasts bare, their faces running with blood. At the same time, in another corner of the room, a young man of about twenty-five was defending himself as best he could from three 'tigresses' who beat him about the face, while several men at the same time belaboured him with sticks. Hickey, alarmed, decided to beat his retreat; but when he tried to open the door the Cerberus, suspecting that he was attempting to escape without paying, grabbed him by the collar and pulled him forcibly back into the room. Later his friends introduced him to another establishment of the same sort—Murphy's (later known as Marjoram's)—a veritable haunt of pickpockets and prostitutes of the lowest type, with a vocabulary coarse enough to shock even Hickey, who believed himself a man of the world.

In reality even at Wetherby's this sort of violence did not take place every night, for when Hickey returned there on another occasion he spent an agreeable evening listening to 'admirable' songs, and one of the singers was a woman called Burgess who had taken part in the fight on his earlier visit, with another woman, Bet Wilkinson, nicknamed 'Blasted Bet'. Again, when he returned to Marjoram's he was highly diverted by Ned Shuter, the comedian, performing in a variety of turns and buffooneries (until the moment, when, dead drunk as always, he was carried off to bed). These are the two faces of London's low life, the one brutal, the other comic, according to circumstances, chance, or the moment in time.

Apart from Wetherby's and Marjoram's, Little Russell Street boasted plenty of other establishments. 'Cross Keys' for example, ostensibly a bathing establishment or 'bagnio', was in fact a brothel. Some of these 'bagnios' were respectable enough, but the majority were houses of call for prostitutes, or else brothels conducted by a 'lady abbess' and stocked with 'nymphs', as they were called. The lot of these girls was not a happy one; the mother abbess usually kept back from each of them a sum of anything between two and five guineas a week to pay for the lodging and clothes she hired them. Some of the houses were run with coloured women; in 1774 the staff of one brothel consisted entirely of negresses.

THE 'LITERATURE' OF PLEASURE

The world of love was the theme of a variety of publications. 'The courtesan's trade', Grosley tells us, 'is so far from being considered as unlawful, that the list of those who are any way eminent is publicly cried about the streets; this list, which is very numerous, points out their places of abode, and gives the most circumstantial and exact detail of their features, their stature and the several qualifications for which they are remarkable. A new one is published every year, and sold under the piazza of Covent Garden, with the title of the *New Atlantis*, and the name of the author, Mr Harris, in the title-page.'

The *New Atlantis* mentioned by Grosley had also been published under the title of *Harris's List of Covent Garden Ladies*, and again as *The Man of Pleasure's Kalendar for the Year*. There were other publications of the same nature: *Nocturnal Revels* was a guide to the houses of pleasures in 1779. Others were designed to divert as well as to catalogue: *The Rambler's Magazine,* for example, and the *Ranger's Magazine* (both illustrated with appropriate plates), the *Bon Ton Magazine,* etc.

All these publications devoted much space to flagellation and indicated those establishments where it could be practised.

OUT OF BOUNDS

The English did not draw the line at flagellation or the pursuit of little girls whose immaturity sometimes held for them more attraction than fully developed charms. Homosexuality had been in practice for some time, and the names of its exponents were often known. One day in the Rotunda at Ranelagh Grosley was with friends who drew his attention to a 'couple' composed of a young man and an old soldier in uniform. In England, of course (as in most European countries), sodomy was punishable by death. As a rule when scandals of this nature broke, those involved, especially those in high places, sought salvation by fleeing to Europe. Lord Tylney was forced to live out his days in Italy, and in 1781 Edward Onslow fled these shores, never to return. The author of *Vathek,* William Beckford, was forced into exile in 1784, and although he returned to England a few years later, it was to live in almost complete isolation. One of the most startling of scandals was that of the 'White Swan'.

Ostensibly a drinks-shop, in reality a house of call for male homosexuals, the 'White Swan' was situated in Vere Street, not far from Clare Market. In one room there were four beds where several couples could be accommodated at the same time; nearby was a room containing all the necessary equipment for the toilet and make-up of clients. Finally there was a 'chapel' where 'marriages' could be celebrated. The regular clients were known under pseudonyms: 'Kitty Cambric' was a coal-merchant; 'Miss Selina', a police officer; 'Black-eyed Leonora', a drummer. Other trades were represented: a butcher, 'Beautiful Henrietta'; 'Lady Godiva', a coffee-house waiter, a gentleman's valet, the 'Duchess of Gloucester'; the 'Duchess of Devonshire' was a blacksmith; 'Miss Soft-Lips', a grocer. The list is notably free of aristocratic names, for homosexuality was by no means a prerogative of the upper classes, in spite of the impression given by the highly publicized scandals of the day.

One Sunday, however, in July 1810, the 'White Swan' was raided by police and thirty-three people were arrested. On Monday morning they were taken by cab from prison to be interrogated at Bow Street. Two months later they were condemned to sentences of up to three years. Some time later a drummer and a lieutenant came before the justices for the same offence, and this time the sentence was death. All had first to undergo the pillory, where they were greatly injured and disfigured by the various missiles with which they were pelted by the crowd; dead cats, rotten eggs, potatoes, mud, buckets filled with fish-guts, blood, excrement, offal from the slaughter-houses. Even bricks were thrown. Some of them had their heads broken; many lost consciousness. These missiles—apples, potatoes, cabbages, turnips, dead cats and dogs—were bought by the mob from astute hawkers (these there have always been), at exorbitant prices.

PART FIVE

RELIGIOUS LIFE

CHAPTER ONE

THE ESTABLISHED PROTESTANT
CHURCH

When George III came to the throne the prevailing religion was
still the 'established' church. The Church of England alone enjoyed official recognition, but since by reason of its episcopal
structure bishops and archbishops were appointed by the Crown,
the ecclesiastical hierarchy found itself dependent on the Government and frequently in its service. 'The Alliance of Church and
State', the title of an imposing volume published in 1741 by Bishop
Warburton, was indeed an alliance of sorts, but one of the allies,
the Church, had to surrender a large part of its autonomy in
exchange for its privileged position. When in 1717 a group of
Churchmen wished to show some independence, the general
assembly—the Convocation—was silenced until 1852, apart from
one fruitless attempt on its part to rise up in 1741.

The causes of the weakness of the Church of England lay to a
great extent within its structure and composition, both of which
clearly reflected the inequality of the society from which it arose.
The position of the curate was usually insecure compared with
that of the vicar, whose duties he often undertook. Further, the
differences in revenue received by the various dioceses, and by the
individual livings within the dioceses, were very great. But it is
hardly possible to offer a generalized account of the ecclesiastical
way of life. Let us, rather, consider in close-up some representative
parsons. First then a parson in need.

WILLIAM JONES, HIS MISFORTUNES, HIS WIFE

The Reverend William Jones, first vicar, then rector of the
parish of Broxbourne from 1780 to 1812, was also a schoolmaster.
His was a hard life, and his expenditure, modest as it was, was
twice his income. In 1799, on the 29 June, this conscientious clergyman wrote: 'I am now in the nineteenth year of my servitude . . .
and to the very best of my recollection or my clerk's, two or at most

143

three Sundays are all that I have have ever been absent from my parish in all that time.'

But Jones had an enemy in the village. Not the squire, for there was none in this parish, but a fat farmer, one of those 'mushroommen' as they were called, who had been enriched by the rise in the prices of agricultural produce. Farmer Rogers was a hard, authoritarian man who would brook no contradiction, and persecuted the unfortunate vicar unremittingly. In 1801, when the living at last fell vacant, Rogers did all he could to prevent Jones from being appointed to it, even going so far as to address to the Bishop of London (who was responsible for the appointment) a letter full of slanderous accusations. Fortunately Rogers did not succeed, but he revenged himself in various petty ways: moving fences surrounding the church, encroaching upon the graveyard, cutting the bell-ropes so that the new incumbent could not be rung in. It is pleasing to hear that in the end Rogers was deprived of his churchwardenship, fined for assaulting a pregnant woman, and died wretchedly on December 20, 1803.

But alas, Jones's troubles were not yet over. He was married to Theodosia, a woman who does not seem to have been a model spouse. Her waspish nature drove William to write a work called *Book of Domestic Lamentations*. Theodosia was the daughter of a lawyer and so expert in sophistry that poor Jones was always worsted in any discussion between them. She reproached him continually for their poverty and forced him to go on teaching, although he would have preferred to live more frugally and to study and improve his mind. Generous to the end, Jones destroyed his *Book of Lamentations* before he died.

William Jones was a deeply religious man. He had placed his own coffin before him in his study, and through the window of his room he could look out upon the yew-tree under which he hoped eventually to be buried.

There was nothing morbid in these arrangements; they simply expressed the thoughts of a Christian convinced of the vanity of human affairs, like the good Doctor Primrose in *The Vicar of Wakefield*. Like him Jones had no fear of death although he loved life: 'How happy, how very happy, do I feel myself in this dear little room. . . . I am undisturbed, I have my cheerful little fire, my books and in short every comfort which I can reasonably desire. I read, I reflect, I write, and endeavour to enjoy as far as I

The Gin shop (Rowlandson)

can that blessed leisure and absence of care with which the good providence of my Heavenly Father has indulged me.' Of his nine children, three daughters and his sailor son had turned out badly. Poor and persecuted, invincibly good-humoured, profoundly optimistic, Jones was in many ways the very image of the Vicar of Wakefield—but with additional characteristics which remind one of Fielding's Parson Adams in *Joseph Andrews*.

THE SQUIRE IN THE CASSOCK

Doctor John Taylor, Samuel Johnson's friend, gives us a very different view. Vicar of Bosworth (where Johnson had once been a schoolmaster), and Prebendary of Westminster, he spent most of his time at Ashbourne, a little Derbyshire town where he was the incumbent. In 1776, hearing that Johnson and the faithful Boswell were on their way to Lichfield, he sent out to fetch them in his great postchaise, drawn by four spanking horses and escorted by two 'jolly' postilions. Let us read Boswell's own description of their arrival at Ashbourne:

'We found Doctor Taylor, quite at his ease in a house at the end of Ashbourne, to which he has built an Octagon room, ten feet each lozenge or division, stuccoed and gilded. He has behind his house some pretty ground, a river, deer, horses and cows. He has £1,000 a year in the Church, and I understood more of land rent. He is an excellent Justice of the Peace; and has a considerable political interest, which he gives to the Devonshire Family. He is like the Father or Sovereign of Ashbourne. He last winter gave away £200 among its inhabitants who were in want of assistance. He keeps a good deal of land in his own hand, breeds horses and remarkable large cattle and game fowls. He has no wit, but as Doctor Johnson observed, a very strong understanding. His second wife was an unreasonable woman, and they have been parted many years. He had an upper servant in a kind of purple dress and large white wig, like the Butler of a Bishop. Peters was his name. We dined well, and I drank a bottle of port.'

And Boswell completes the portrait of Doctor Taylor: 'His size and figure and countenance and manner were that of a hearty English squire, with the parson superimposed.'

K

This combination of squire and parson was so familiar in the eighteenth century that in the end a special word was coined to describe him: he was known as the 'squarson'. William Cowper hit him off in the mordant phrase: 'the huntsman in a surplice', while Crabbe fixed him in the following spirited lines:

> A jovial youth, who thinks his Sunday's task
> As much as God or man can fairly ask;
> The rest he gives to loves and labours light,
> To fields the morning and to feasts the night;
> None better skill'd the noisy pack to guide
> To urge their chase, to cheer them or to chide;
> A sportsman keen he shoots through half the day,
> And skill'd at whist, devotes the night to play.

Clearly then the life of a typical country parson like James Woodforde, with money of his own, was not fundamentally very different from this, even if it took a rather different form. No one could possibly accuse Woodforde of neglecting his pastoral duties; nevertheless it is surprising, all things taken into consideration, to see how little place they occupied in everyday life, and how little thought he gave to them. His way of life, being more or less typical, is worth examining more closely.

THE REVEREND JAMES WOODFORDE'S COMFORTABLE LIFE

James Woodforde was born in 1740—the son of a clergyman. He went to Winchester, and from there to Oxford where he became a fellow of New College. He served as curate in a number of parishes in the West of England, mostly in Somerset, until in 1773 he returned to Oxford. There he held a variety of posts, and was also received as a freemason into Alfred Lodge—the University Lodge (there was another for the town, the Constitutional Lodge). In 1774 he was presented with the living of the parish of Weston Longeville in Norfolk, where he dwelt from 1776 to 1802.

Parson Woodforde's diary, which covers a period of forty-four years, is revealing in that it deals with so few topics. Woodforde treats us untiringly to detailed menus of his meals, not only of the ones of which he partook when invited out to dine, but of those of everyday, which to us seem prodigious; they remained plentiful, even during the years of general food shortage between 1796 and 1800. Such exercise as Woodforde took, fishing or frequently hunting hares, seems to have been insufficient to rid him of the effects of the vast quantities of food he swallowed. Thus he became a martyr to gout at quite an early age—an affliction which he treated by dosing himself with a bottle or two of port wine.

At home in the evenings or at the house of the squire, with whom he was on good terms, he played cards for money as did everyone else, but with only moderate stakes. From time to time he travelled to Norwich to stay for short periods, or even to the West Country where the rest of his family lived.

Woodforde is full of information about his farming activities and his differences with recalcitrant farmers who allowed their beasts to stray into his meadows; about the income his tithes brought in; about his pig-breeding. There are frequent references such as: 'The old sow gave birth to sixteen piglets . . .' and 'Nancy's pig was killed this morning and a nice fine fat white pig it is. It is to be weighed tomorrow morning. We are to make some Somersett black puddings tomorrow.' One day one of his finest animals drank the grounds from a beer barrel. It was odd that a few years later the same thing should happen to some pigs belonging to the Reverend Sydney Smith, when he fed them fermented grain, whereupon, we are told, they expressed their appreciation by grunting out the tune of the national anthem. Woodforde's animals did not go as far as this, but the parson carefully observed their uncoordinated movements. Woodforde's beer was, indeed, locally famous. He brewed it himself of course, and every time he prepared a barrel of strong beer it kept the whole household busy for two full days. Even the local farmers had to admit they had never drunk such good beer elsewhere.

Religion as such occupies very little space in Woodforde's diary, and his record of Church affairs is limited to altercations with choristers and the distribution of livings. Woodforde held a service every Sunday, either in the morning *or* the afternoon, and celebrated communion as did most of his fellow clergy, four times a year. Apart from Sundays the only service he held was on Good Friday. He visited the sick and gave alms to the poor. The only prayer mentioned in the length and breadth of his record of forty-four years is on March 8, 1789, when he read a thanksgiving for the return to health of His Majesty. His private devotions reveal nothing but his fears of bad omens and plagues. Crabbe's words aptly describe him:

> He was his Master's soldier but not one
> To lead an army of his martyrs on. . . .

Even under George III there were parsons who led more heroic lives than Woodforde. But there were others who were even more deeply sunk in material affairs. Certainly after a convivial evening he can write with evident delight: 'We were all very merry and very harmonious', and 'we were very merry—a bottle was passed round'—(in the eighteenth century the word 'merry' was a euphemism; Woodforde's pigs were frankly 'drunk', but their owner was merely 'merry'). But he was at least always sober for a funeral.

This did not apply to a certain ecclesiastic who, we are told, was so drunk that he collapsed into the very grave he was blessing. Nor to the Reverend Shipton who, his fellow clergyman, the Reverend William Cole, tells us, was so far gone in his cups that he had to be put to bed. Nor was Woodforde really like the Vicar of Loughton who was accused of slipping his hand when drunk up the skirt of his maidservant and offering her five guineas if she would sleep with him. Or the Reverend John Thomlinson (author of a number of reputable sermons) who records in his journal that after an unsuccessful attempt to seduce one of his parishioners, he was about to 'try' another, whom he might, if hearsay about her were true, manage to take by force.

The slightly bellicose behaviour of some of these ecclesiastics sometimes manifested itself in more dangerous form. One of Woodforde's neighbours, the Reverend Beevor, was arrested in 1801 for challenging an officer to a duel. In 1782 Pastor Moritz records that one of his English colleagues fought a duel with pistols in Hyde Park and killed his adversary. At this period too the Reverend Bate Dudley was famous for his duelling and for his frequent use of fisticuffs to which he owed his nickname of 'the fighting parson'. Nevertheless those who attracted public attention in this way remained exceptional, especially among the lower ranks of the clergy. Most of these were wise enough to remember the maxim of George Crabbe:

> Vicars must with discretion go astray,
> Whilst bishops may be damn'd the nearest way

THE CLERK

The parson was generally assisted by his clerk, who, to judge by William Cowper's observations, had an important part to play: 'Not only must the clerk pronounce the *Amen* to prayers and announce the sermon. He must also be universal father to those he guides to the altar and he is godfather to every new-born babe.'

In fact the clerk's duties were even more numerous. It was he who led the chants and gave the responses; he kept the accounts, registered baptisms, marriages and burials; he saw that the surplices were laundered, chased dogs out of church and forced unwilling youngsters in; he was also responsible for cleaning.

In return for all this the clerk received £2 a year, to which were added marriage and funeral expenses and various perquisites. He was so indispensable that most vicars preferred to shut their eyes to any weaknesses of character. Thus William Cole could write of his own clerk that he was 'A quiet, good-tempered man, and no fault but drunkenness. . . . He had been drunk for a week together, and was so drunk this morning that I was sent to, to desire that Will Turpin might officiate as Clerk (he being Sexton).' Woodforde's clerk was a 'good-for-nothing' who could neither sing nor be trusted to take collection. But he must have been surpassed by a clerk of Broxbourne parish. When the Reverend William Jones was appointed to the living he was surprised to find that the ancient parchments—records of baptisms, marriages, and deaths had disappeared; the sacristan explained that the clerk, a tailor by trade, had cut them into fine strips to enable him to take his customers' measurements.

CHURCH BUILDINGS

In the reign of George III the clergy often endeavoured to repair churches in bad condition. The simplest way to give them a respectable appearance was to whitewash their walls. Contemporary thought tended to justify this practice in terms of the light of reason shining to dispel the shades of mysticism and ignorance. Whatever the truth behind this symbolic interpretation, the result of the practice was the 'flood of whitening' denounced anonymously in the *The Gentleman's Magazine* of 1799, and which was so irritating to Beckford that he poured scorn upon his own architect, 'the villain' Wyatt, who, he said, in his attempts to restore Salisbury Cathedral had reduced it to poorness:

'. . . bare and insipid, without mystery, without ecclesiastical pomp. . . . Oh the disgust and stink of Protestantism (it doesn't deserve the sonorous name of Heresy). All these windows, all this light, all this glass with its small diamond-shaped panes make this shameless church look like a whore clad only in muslin— What an infamous spot. How I abhor it. . . .'

Despite the extravagance of his words, the hermit of Fonthill was not so far wrong. Had Joseph Butler, the Bishop of Durham, not been formerly accused of Papist leanings when he had put up a stained glass window in his cathedral? Had not the King himself opposed those who proposed to adorn the interior of St Paul's with painting? Beckford's indignation was in fact an explosion of that romanticism, with its love of colour, stained glass, deep shadow, of mystery and mysticism—all things which the Church of England on the whole failed to offer, and even refused to offer the faithful. Yet millions of Englishmen remained fast to this reasonable and moderate Church. Why? Undoubtedly one reason is that it was so much bound up in the everyday life of the people.

THE CHURCH AND LIFE

It would be incorrect to represent the Church of England as being entirely without religious influence, at least in those places where it was represented. The books which sold best all through this century were three works which expressed the Anglican view, regardless of their individual differences: a manual of devotion entitled *The Duty of Mankind*, Archbishop Tillotson's *Sermons*, William Law's *A Serious call to a devout and Holy Life*. Besides these and together with a Bible, every Anglican family possessed its own prayer book in which the names and dates of birth of the children, and the date of their parents' marriage were written down: the Prayer Book of the Church of England was an integral part of the family's religious life. In the countryside particularly the Church was closely bound up with the lives of the people: not only did it celebrate with religious ceremonies the great events of family life, but it held in its registers the actual records of the State. Furthermore, whenever an offence against the moral code was committed, the delinquent of either sex was forced to do penance in public; summoned to appear in Church at the time appointed for Divine Service, bareheaded and barefooted, the offender, draped in a white sheet, staff in hand, would confess his crime aloud and beg forgiveness. This practice was still current under George III, particularly when a child was born out of wedlock: in village communities the parents submitted to this treatment, it seems, with fairly good grace.

RELIGIOUS SERVICES

Yet there were hardly ever any daily services. In most parishes there were only Sunday services, sometimes two, more often one. In Nettlebed where Pastor Moritz passed through one Sunday, the service was due to begin at nine-thirty. Moritz was impressed by the village children 'lined up all bright and beautiful' like recruits, at the end of the village street. 'Very nice and clean, and their hair (cut round in a fringe after the English fashion) combed.' They shone with health, 'the white collars of their shirts were turned back at both sides and their breasts were open to the air'. When the parson arrived on his horse 'the boys took off their hats and bowed low to him'. Then the bell rang to call the congregation. The church was quite simple inside: above the altar were displayed the Ten Commandments in large letters on two tablets . . . under the pulpit was a reading-desk where the preacher stood before the sermon and read out a very long liturgy. The clerk made the responses and the congregation joined in in whispers. The service included a sermon, psalms, and two lessons. The clerk said: 'Let us praise God' and the congregation joined in singing the anthem 'Awake our hearts, awake with joy.' The anthem was accompanied by several musical instruments; after the psalms the parson stood up and announced the text of the sermon: 'Not all who say Lord, Lord, shall enter into the Kingdom of Heaven.' He dealt with the subject so clearly and with such conviction and sincerity that Pastor Moritz was 'often touched to tears'.

A very different scene is described for us a few years later, in 1787, this time by an Englishman. It refers to a small village some twenty miles from London, the name of which is not mentioned.

'The houses were much scattered about, and appeared beggarly; but within sight of the church there stood a gentleman's seat, which was laid out with all the elegance that could be bestowed upon the house and grounds. The churchyard joined to the park. Having surveyed every thing there, it being Sunday, I went into the church; to which one miserable bell, much like a small porridge-pot, called half a dozen people, which number comprehended the congregation. The churchyard itself was low and wet; a broken gate the entrance; a few small wooden tombs and an old yew-tree the only ornaments. The inside of the church answered the outside; the walls green with damp; a few broken benches; with pieces of mats, dirty and very ragged; the stairs to the pulpit half worn away; the communion-table stood upon three legs; the rails worm-eaten and half gone. The minister of this noble edifice was answerable to it in dress and manners. Having entered the church, he made the best of his way to the chancel, where he changed his wig, put on a dirty, iron-mouled, ragged surplice, and, after a short angry dialogue with the clerk, entered his desk, and began immediately without looking into the book. He read as if he had ten other churches to serve that day, at as many miles distance from each other. The clerk sung a melancholy solo; neither tune nor words of which I ever heard before. Then followed a short, confused, hurried discourse; after this the small congregation departed; which had consisted of a gentleman and his family from the distance of about a mile and a half, and two old men, who constantly attended for sixpence apiece, given by that family. The door was then shut, till the next Sunday came round.'

The description may be biased, but it is nevertheless true that in many places church singing had deteriorated, since many parsons looked upon hymn-singing as a survival of popery. In 1790 Beigly Porteous, the Bishop of London, wrote: 'Psalmody is now almost totally useless to the Church of England.' During the eighteenth century the singing of hymns revived somewhat, thanks to the dissenters and Methodists. The celebration of Communion was infrequent: in most parishes no more than four times a year—at Easter, Whitsun, Michaelmas and Christmas. The sacraments were often given at the altar, but sometimes elsewhere, at a table put up especially for the purpose: communicants did not invariably kneel to receive them. On the whole the most important element of the service was the sermon.

THE SERMON

Under the Stuarts and until 1688 preachers were often reproached for the 'learnedness' of their oratory, with its garnish of Greek and Latin phrases and its ostentatious rhetoric. By 1765 Goldsmith was complaining that he heard nothing but dry, methodical and cold sermons delivered with placid insipidity. He protested against the sort of 'peaceful' preachers who appeared to be addressing a cushion under their noses rather than a church full of people. Such complaints were made in vain; the age of reason and enlightenment had succeeded the century of brilliance, originality and profound perception.

Ten years later Doctor Thomas Campbell, the Irish parson, visited London and thought little of the service at the Temple. The sermon, he said 'was the most meagre composition (on our Saviour's temptation)', and the manner of delivery was even worse. The preacher stood stockstill holding his text as though it were a newspaper. His delivery was slow and devoid of elegance and nuance. On the same evening Campbell listened to a sermon in Westminster Abbey—'still duller and as ill delivered'. Pastor Moritz, although agreeably impressed by English piety, had to admit that the tone of the preachers was monotonous and lacking in passion.

Parsons often made use of collections of sermons, composed once and for all, allowing no scope for improvisation. In 1762 Parson Woodforde on a visit to Somerset refused an invitation to stand in for the vicar for the Sunday service: 'I could not, as I brought no sermon with me.' Other parsons would have been less conscientious, perhaps substituting a sermon from one of these collections. Thus Southey could write in 1807: 'It has become a branch of trade to supply the priests with discourses, and sermons may be bespoken upon any subject. . . .' According to his account there were centres which furnished sermons to order, and at prices varying with the social status of the congregation for which they were intended. In fact most preachers were content to draw on existing collections using the whole text or extracts from it. The novelist Sterne was no more scrupulous than others in this respect. These collections were guaranteed to sell: in 1806 when Sydney Smith needed cash for the expenses of moving to a new living, he managed to get £200 for his published sermons.

In 1778 Doctor Johnson advised preachers not to model their

discourse on that of Archbishop Tillotson, with his simple, elegant and straightforward delivery. And yet, throughout the length of the eighteenth century Tillotson continued to inspire sermons which preached humanity and benevolence above all else, in which, William Jones remarked, the name of Christ was hardly ever mentioned. The spirit that moved Tillotson to take as his text for one sermon: 'His commandments are not grievous' had not died with him in 1694. Thus in 1763 Boswell noted in his journal that he had heard an 'excellent sermon' with the title 'My yoke is light to bear'. And in 1789 a letter addressed to the *Gentleman's Magazine* outlined the sermon given one Sunday in a little village church. The Almighty was pictured as a being of 'boundless beneficence' who had created Man with his happiness in view and multiplied his sources of enjoyment:

'Shame to those teachers of a severe and gloomy creed, who paint the Supreme Being in the horrid colours of their own distempered minds or vitiated hearts! Look there my children, examine your own hearts, they will teach that the great end of your existence is to be happy yourselves and to contribute to the happiness of your fellow-creatures. . . . Be ye virtuous; be active in your several occupations; be not envious of those that are above you, for they have their cares which are greater than yours; be affectionate and charitable one towards another. Love as the father of mercies. Be happy here, and trust in his infinite mercy for your eternal happiness hereafter.'

Sermons of this kind infuriated the puritans and all those who had fallen under the influence of Calvinism. But outside these circles, which in the first years of the reign were in any case relatively few, they reflected the tendency of the Church of England to place the emphasis on behaviour and morality rather upon doctrine. Nevertheless dissent already existed, and its influence was by no means negligible.

CHAPTER TWO

DISSENTING PROTESTANTS

Chief among the original dissenters were the Presbyterians, the Independents (later to be called Congregationalists), and the Baptists and the Quakers. Despite individual variations of doctrines and dogma, all these sects or denominations had one thing in common: refusal to recognize the episcopalian structure of the Church of England. Numerically the Quakers were undoubtedly the most important group. The diocese of York for example, for which we possess statistics recorded by Archbishop Herring, seems to have been fairly typical; and here the Presbyterians owned seventy chapels or meeting-houses, the Independents twenty, the Baptists twenty and the Quakers one hundred.

The adherents of these various beliefs suffered from certain discriminatory measures; they might not be elected to Parliament, nor admitted to the universities. They set up their own teaching establishments which were known as 'academies', where instruction was invariably given by their own clergy. The Government shut its eyes to various subterfuges whereby these believers could be admitted to official posts, by 'occasional conformity' to Anglican rites. But sometimes their election to municipal responsibilities amounted to a form of persecution: they could be condemned equally for accepting posts of this kind, since no dissenter had the right to do so, or for refusing, since no good citizen was supposed to be able to escape from responsibilities of this kind. One of their main grievances was that they were obliged to pay dues to the Church of England in particular tithes.

In fact the sects had lost the greater part of their earlier fighting spirit. Their exclusion from Parliament and public posts in itself served to draw them towards other lucrative branches of activity offered by the economic development in the country, in particular to industry and banking. The role of the Quakers appears to have been preponderant in these two realms (and mainly in metallurgy).

THE QUAKERS

Visitors from France who often described their meetings were usually struck by the calm and contemplative mood and by the charm of the women. Thus M. Grosley in 1765:

'. . . the beauty of most of the sex, set off by English neatness, is further heightened by the simplicity of their dress; their linen, their robes, their hats, are all plain, without any sort of ornament; this does not prevent such as are rich (and almost all of them are so), from wearing the finest linen, and being very particular on the choice of their stuffs, which are, however, of modest colours.'

Thirty years later Faujas de Saint-Fond felt very much the same. Invited to supper with a Quaker friend, he noticed that the women in the company

'. . . were neither powdered nor perfumed, and had not, like most ladies, heads full of feathers, or artificial flowers; but their beautiful hair floated with becoming gracefulness on handkerchiefs uncommonly white and fine. The chief attraction of their simple but elegant dress lay in the beauty and excellent quality of the stuffs which composed it, and above all in the charming faces and the grace of those who wore it.'

According to Faujas, everything in the house was in keeping with 'the exquisite simplicity' which characterized the Quakers.

The table, for instance, was in no way austere. Although there were no napkins, this was not peculiar to the Quakers. The meal itself consisted of delicious food served in elegant dishes.

'The cloth was removed at the dessert, and fruits, comfits, and other delicacies, with a variety of wines, in crystal decanters, were placed on a table of the finest mahogany. This is the luxury of the English. We drank more than once in champagne and claret, to the health of our fair companions, and they pledged us in madeira and constance. . . . Tea, punch, and fine liqueurs came in their turn. We should have passed the whole night at table, had we yielded to the pressing invitations of the doctor. But notwithstanding we left the party at one o'clock in the morning.'

156

'And,' adds Faujas, 'during the remainder of the night I meditated how I should become a Quaker. . . .'

The halls at Quaker meetings were as clean as their houses: 'The walls are of a dazzling white, the wainscoting, unencumbered with sculpture, shines in the modest lustre of its natural colours, and the exquisite cleanliness with which it is kept; the seats are simple benches, placed in parallel rows . . . when the Quakers are assembled in their churches, the men occupy a place apart from that of the women, and have their heads covered with a black hat, of a broad half-cocked brim, without loop or button; their eyes are cast humbly to the ground. . . . The women also have their heads covered with bonnets of a different kind, in silk, velvet or straw, but very plain. . . . Their hair, too, is without powder but is washed and trimmed with such neatness that it forms one of their finest ornaments. . . . At the farther end of the church there is a kind of platform, a little raised, and surrounded with a wooden balustrade: it is not a pulpit; it is rather a large and long tribune from which to harangue.' Those who felt inspired could take the floor. It was at this moment of inspiration that Faujas, watching them 'through a glass' saw them: 'their eyes half shut, or bent toward the ground, while slowly, and at long intervals, they pronounce some words in a sad and melancholy tone; they then sway backwards and forwards, sometimes sideways; at first with a slow and uniform motion, uttering some words more rapidly. Their action then redoubles: and this struggle of body and mind soon drives the blood towards the head; the cheeks redden, a crowd of thoughts arises, expressions follow; the whole soul and heart are kindled; a sort of quaking appears, and the orator is inspired.' Many of these orations, according to Faujas, 'are below mediocrity, some are tolerable; it is even said that some are very eloquent'; on one occasion Faujas overheard a woman improvising 'a very fine prayer to God' in which was a 'fine emotion of love and gratitude'. 'Women,' declares the Frenchman, 'will always give us lessons in this respect.'

When George III came to the throne, the former violent demonstrations of hostility towards the Quakers and some other dissenters had to a great extent subsided. Hostile feelings now tended to be concentrated more forcibly upon the Methodists who, in any case, were regarded by the Anglican church as the most harmful of the established sects, even though the animosity against them was also less violent than it had been twenty years earlier.

THE METHODISTS

The Methodist teaching which underlay various internal divergences of opinion (John Wesley and George Whitefield representing the two main drifts of opinion within the movement), insisted on the supreme importance of faith. It sought not to fight the Church of England, but rather to regenerate it from within, by increasing the number of religious services, by initiating services in the many parishes where none were held, and above all by restoring the primacy of faith, by opposing the conception of religion as a political instrument with the conception of a truly religious Church.

The Anglican clergy on their side reproached the Methodists for preaching outside the churches and for holding their own meetings and for appealing to personal inspiration—'enthusiasm' —as the principal element in worship. By the beginning of the reign the persecution had lost much of its violence: the period when the lord of the manor and the Anglican parson had incited the mob to stone Methodist preachers was past (these activities were to recommence with the French Revolution), aimed this time not against the Methodists who tended towards conservative policies, but against the Presbyterians or the Independents, who were often in sympathy with the principles of 1789. But hostility from the official Church as a whole remained.

Wesley endeavoured for as long as he could to remain within the body of the established church. It was only on September 1, 1784, when faced with the ill will of the Anglican hierarchy, which was refusing to ordain Wesleyan preachers for America, that John Wesley made up his mind to ordain two of them himself, first as deacons, then as ministers; and then in 1785 for Scotland, and during 1788–89 for those parts of England where the established clergy were refusing the Sacraments to the Methodists, he ordained more ministers. After Wesley's death the separation became final. The founder of Methodism had, only against his will and under the force of circumstances, turned to a solution which inevitably transformed what had originally been merely a religious society into a Church. Even in 1791 the Methodists were still known, more

158

often than not, as 'Mr Wesley's people', in the same way that the small Calvinist following led by Whitefield in the first period of the movement had been known as 'the Group' or 'Lady Huntingdon's Connexion', from the name of the noble woman who had supported the Methodist movement from its earliest beginnings.

The 'Society' was divided into groups of eleven people, known as 'classes' and placed under the guidance of a 'leader'; each person contributed a penny a week; the class brought together anyone who had shown 'the wish to flee from the Divine wrath'. A more exclusive group—'band'—existed, to unite those who, already 'regenerate', were on their way to perfect Christianity. The entire organization was split up into 'circuits' under Wesley's leadership as 'superintendent'. Each circuit was directed by an 'assistant', who in his turn became 'superintendent'.

The original purpose of their meetings was to discuss matters of common interest, but they soon turned into prayer meetings, at which it became customary to confess one's sins. There was hymn-singing too (of which we shall have more to say later), and an entire liturgy was gradually developed. There were 'preaching services' and 'love feasts', at first reserved to members of the 'bands', and later enlarged to include every member of the Society; at these feasts a piece of cake was eaten and a glass of water drunk by all present, in token of brotherhood and solidarity. On the first Sunday of the year there was a special Covenant service. The words of the pact which all Christians must make with their Lord were read aloud; each then signified his submission and then prayed that his own individual pact might be ratified in Heaven.

John Wesley's brother, Charles, made a major contribution to the development of the Methodist hymnal. Nowadays the words of these hymns sometimes make us smile: 'Raise dying earthworms to the sky', or 'The worms of earth attempt to sing Thy praises'. But the tunes, taken from Purcell or from German church music, or even out of contemporary opera, were invariably well put together and for this reason alone have today been put aside in favour of easier and simpler tunes of less distinction. Various collections were published before the definitive edition of 1780, which included not only hymns by Charles Wesley (he alone wrote more than 6,000), but also by others, among them Isaac Watts. Some of these, particularly ones which celebrate the birth of Christ, are amongst those most often sung by Anglicans today.

159

On September 27, 1787 John Wesley, now eighty-four, arrived at Castle Cary (the parish in Somerset which Parson Woodforde had served from 1765 to 1773). He wrote in his *Journal*: 'How are the times changed! The first of our preachers that came hither, the zealous mob threw into the horse-pond. Now high and low earnestly listen to the word that is able to save their souls.' Four years later, by the time of his death, there were tens of thousands of people whose lives had been changed by the preaching of Wesley and his friends. Many of them felt as did John Nelson, the mason from Yorkshire, who had many times proved himself in service of the cause: 'I was like a wandering bird, cast out of the nest, till Mr John Wesley came to preach his first sermon in Moorfields. . . . When he had done, I thought, "This man can tell the secrets of my heart; but he hath not left me there, for he hath showed the remedy, even the blood of Jesus".'

By 1791 not only had the Methodists increased their following and moved towards the goal of Christian perfection, they had also raised the social status of the movement. The virtues of sincerity, determination, hard work, solidarity and sobriety which they had displayed in the pursuit of their ideal had simultaneously helped to enrich many of their number. John Wesley, writing in 1787, was conscious of the fact that things had changed, and he wrote in his *Journal*: 'For the Methodists in every place grow diligent and frugal: consequently they increase in goods. Hence they proportionably increase in pride, in anger, in the desire of the flesh, the desire of the eyes, and the pride of life. So, although the form of religion remains, the spirit is swiftly vanishing away.' It seems that this bourgeois feeling within the movement caused some anxiety to Wesley in his old age, yet it was inevitable and certainly irreversible.

THE EVANGELICALS

Like Methodism, the Evangelical movement sought to regenerate faithful Anglicans, but unlike Methodism it never alienated itself from the established Church. There were other differences too: apart from some glaring exceptions, Methodism grew originally from out of the lower classes, while Evangelism was always socially 'respectable' and conservative in its politics. The first difficulties and internal schisms among the Methodists had arisen

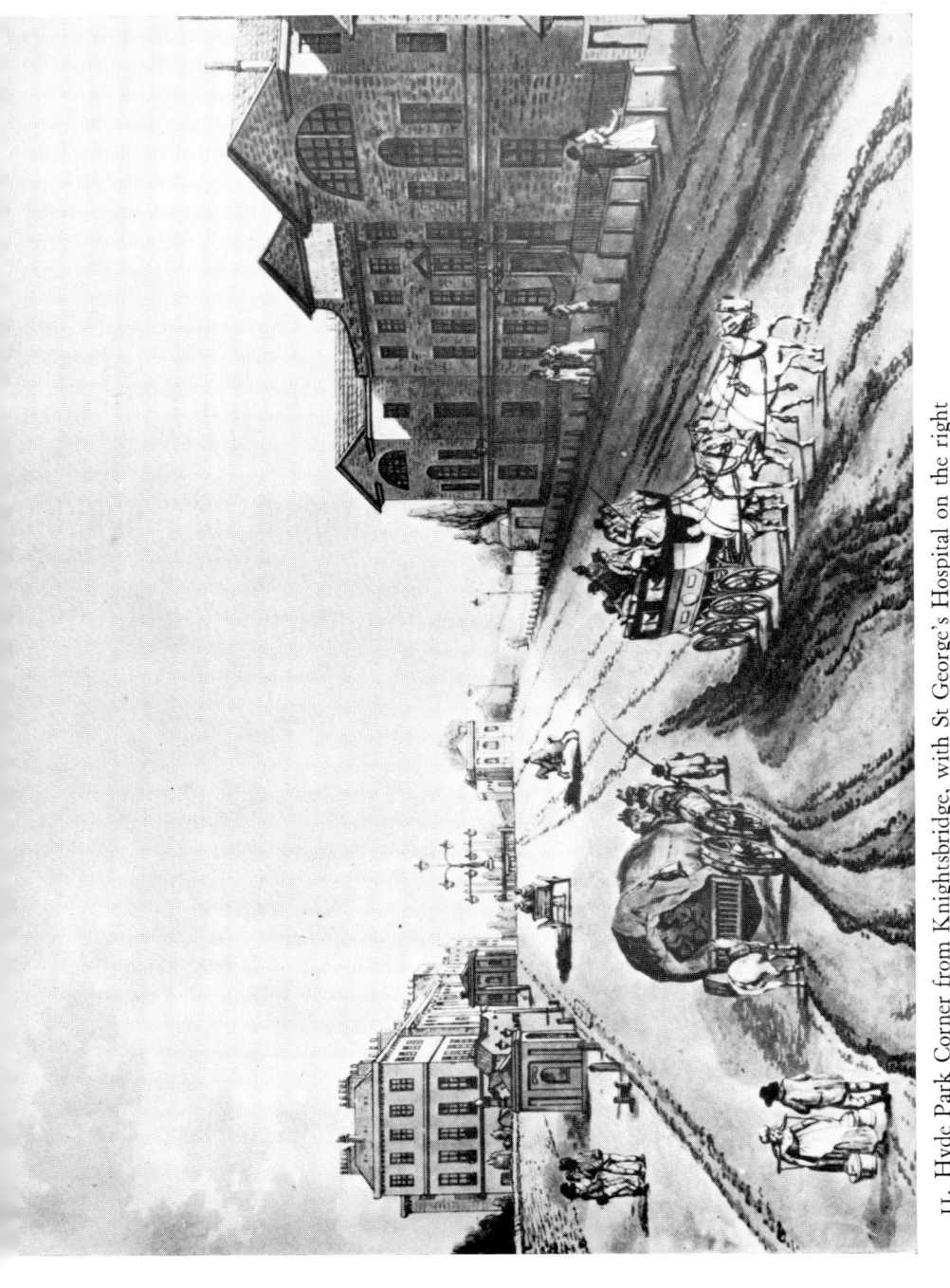

11. Hyde Park Corner from Knightsbridge, with St George's Hospital on the right

12 Hanover Square

from divergences of a theological nature. Nothing comparable occurred within the body of Evangelism, simply because preoccupations of this kind were foreign to the movement. Apart from a belief in the irredeemable depravity of human beings, there was no Evangelical theology: the creed was intellectually void and theologically barren. The Evangelicals were less interested in changing the English conception of religion than in transforming the way of life, not merely of churchgoers, but of all. The main characteristics of the initiators of the movement were distrust of intelligence, hatred of rationalism, emphasis on the emotions and an insistent, sometimes morbid preoccupation with death. From Calvinism they drew the concept of the total fall of the human race, and from Puritanism their condemnation of card playing, the theatre, dancing, and every form of 'dissipation'.

The first generation of Evangelicals grew up between 1760–80, no doubt influenced by Methodism. Two of their number, William Romaine and Henry Venn, were almoners to the Countess of Huntingdon. Another, Richard Cecil, a descendant of the great Burleigh family, was the son of a London industrialist whose dyeing works operated in conjunction with the East India Company. Two other members, brothers, Isaac and Joseph Milner, had been educated at Cambridge. In addition to members of the ruling classes there were extraordinary figures like John Newton, who had gone to sea when he was eleven years old and after a hard life working in the slave trade, was ordained in 1764, and William Cowper, who himself in his poems shows leaning towards Evangelism. But on the whole this first generation was 'respectable' in its background.

The second generation grew from a still more distinguished milieu: the group known as the 'Clapham sect' now came to play an important part in Evangelism. John Venn, son of Henry Venn, whom we have already mentioned, in 1792 was vicar of the parish of Clapham in the suburbs of South London. The real head of this sect was, however, a personal friend of Pitt, William Wilberforce, who had been born into a rich Yorkshire family in 1759. In 1779 he represented Hull in Parliament, but thirteen years later he went to live in Clapham. Another member of the sect was John Thornton whose father, a rich banker, was likewise Member of Parliament. John gave unstintingly to the cause, purchasing livings in various parishes in order to plant ministers there who were

L

already converted. He distributed the Bible and other edifying works, which he sometimes had printed at his own expense. John's second son, as generous as his father, gave away to the cause six-sevenths of his income before his marriage in 1796, and two-thirds on becoming a minister. Other figures were Thomas Gisborne, parson and squire of his village, and Hannah More the 'blue-stocking', who founded Sunday schools, and published works designed to convert the rich, as well as cheaper works deemed fit for the edification of the poor.

The Evangelicals worked not only individually, but also through a variety of organizations. Thanks to the initiative of Wilberforce, a 'Society for the Implementation of the Royal Proclamation against Vice and Immorality' was inaugurated in 1787. Since the title was so long it soon came to be known as 'The Society for the Proclamation'. Similar societies had been in existence since the beginning of the eighteenth century: but this was the first time that one of them had had at its head, instead of a middle-class devotee, influential figures like the Duke of Montagu and members of the Church hierarchy, such as the Archbishops of Canterbury and York, seventeen bishops and others. Towards the end of the century it was absorbed by the 'Society for the Suppression of Vice', which devoted itself to the denunciation and bringing to court of authors, printers, and publishers of 'obscene' literature (the term was widened to include 'seditious' works), licensees who permitted their premises to be used for dancing, domestic servants who bathed unclothed in the sea at Brighton and elsewhere, and sometimes of odd characters like the fortune teller, Joseph Powell, who was sentenced in 1808 to six months' imprisonment for his trade. The hostility of the Evangelicals was also strongly directed against the theatre. When *Percy*, Hannah More's tragedy written in 1777, was staged ten years later, the author, by this time converted to Evangelism, refused to attend rehearsals of the play. And when a bill was put before Parliament to authorize the opening of a theatre in Birmingham, it was thrown out as a result of the purpose-ful activity of an eminent Evangelical, the Earl of Dartmouth.

CHAPTER THREE

SINGULAR ASPECTS OF RELIGIOUS LIFE

THE ENGLISH SUNDAY

One of the favourite activities of the Evangelicals was their work to ensure observance of the 'sabbath'. In this, however, they were only intensifying and extending a course of action which went back to an earlier day. In 1781 Bishop Porteous had pushed through a bill forbidding amusements of any kind on Sunday evening, including even the meetings of debating societies (more familiarly known as 'spouting clubs'), so widespread in London. Earlier still, in 1765 M. Grosley had depicted the English Sunday in depressing colours (see page 93), and the Prussian Pastor Moritz tells how he was called to order one Sunday by his landlady's son for whistling. Nevertheless it is true to say that on another occasion he had spent Sunday evening at an Oxford tavern, in the company of some fellow clerics, all of them drinking together far into the night—until one of them suddenly remembered he was due to take Mattins that very morning at All Souls'. It seems that members of the clergy were not always so punctilious as some of the laity.

When the German visitor Sophie von La Roche met Mrs Fielding, Lady Finch's daughter and governess to the royal princesses, she suggested that she call upon her on Sunday morning, whereupon Mrs Fielding replied that on Sundays it was not done either to receive or to pay calls. Parson Woodforde was not exactly a fanatic, but, on Sunday morning his razor broke while he was honing it: 'May it always be a warning to me not to shave on the Lord's Day or do any other work to profane it *pro futuro.*'

It would be wrong to conclude that the efforts of the Evangelicals and other societies favouring strictness had no effect on Sunday observance. We have only to read what Southey had to say, writing in 1808, at a time when the movement was particularly energetic:

'The Savoyard, who goes about with his barrel-organ, dares not grind even a psalm-tune upon the sabbath. The old woman who sells apples at the corner of the street has been sent to prison for

163

profanation of the Lord's day, by the Society for the Suppression of Vice; the pastrycook, indeed, is permitted to keep his shop-window half open, because some of the society themselves are fond of iced-creams. Yonder goes a crowd to the Tabernacle, as dismally as if they were going to a funeral; the greater number are women—inquire for their husbands at the ale-house, and you will find them besotting themselves there, because all amusements are prohibited as well as all labour, and they cannot lie down, like dogs, and sleep. Ascend a step higher in society—the children are yawning, and the parents agree that the clock must be too slow, that they may accelerate supper and bed-time. In the highest ranks, indeed, there is little or no distinction of days, except that there is neither theatre nor opera for them, and some among them scruple at cards.'

Although the birth of the Evangelical movement ante-dated the French Revolution, its activities were encouraged by the developments in France. The upheaval of the Revolution clearly showed to what ungodliness could bring a people: democracy was the inevitable consequence of impiety; democracy in the eyes of the eighteenth-century Englishman was synonymous with subversion and anarchy. Thus in 1789 *The Annual Register* described with evident satisfaction the effect of the French Revolution on the Church of England:

'The established clergy were roused to a strenuous recommendation of the Christian doctrines, particularly a due observance of the external order, institutions and usages of the Church of England. The churches were well attended, and sometimes even crowded. It was a wonder to the lower orders, throughout all parts of England, to see the avenues to the churches filled with carriages. This novel appearance prompted the simple country-people to enquire what was the matter.'

This development among the Anglican clergy was to have a consequential effect; they now came more easily to accept the steps taken some years earlier towards Catholic emancipation.

THE CATHOLICS

Since the beginning of the reign many of the Anglican clergy had shut their eyes to the presence of Catholic priests in the neighbourhood of their own churches. The Reverend William Cole in

1767 took offence when questioned by his superiors about the state of Catholics in his parish. Indeed Cole was a great admirer of the Catholic hierarchy, especially in France, for the sense of duty it showed in times of disaster, such as outbreaks of plague. He was deeply dissatisfied with the (according to him) inadequate manner in which his own Bishop performed his duties. Indeed there were many Protestants who, without going as far as this, could adopt an attitude of tolerance towards the Catholics. From 1788 their priests no longer risked prosecution and imprisonment for celebrating Mass. A Catholic son could inherit from his father; and Catholics had the right to purchase real estate. We should not therefore misinterpret the riots provoked in 1780 by the fanatical behaviour of Lord Gordon: these had a social as well as religious significance, since the houses of rich Protestants were sought out for pillage and destruction no less than Catholic homes. Even at their height they amounted to no more than a temporary flare-up of the old anti-Papist feeling, which was to recur. From 1791 the law accorded to Catholics the right to worship. Certainly various discriminatory measures still remained: no Catholic could run a school; Catholic marriages and funerals might only be celebrated in public according to Anglican rites; no Catholic was eligible for promotion to officer in the Army or Navy; no Catholic had the vote. It was not until 1828–29 that all restrictions were done away with.

FREEMASONRY

It was during this reign that English freemasonry developed, on the margin of the Church of England, and closely aligned with it. Freemasonry in its very origins seems to have been a typically British phenomenon. It had made its first appearance towards the middle of the seventeenth century, at a time when the ancient guilds no longer reflected modern economic development, especially in England, and were being transformed, above all in London, into non-professional associations concerned with social, civic and political affairs. Alongside this, freemasonry adopted not only the vocabulary inherited from the ancient guilds, but also their traditional initiation rites, their 'mysteries', and 'secrets', deprived now of their technical and professional significance, and used in a purely symbolical sense. It seems probable that some of the first English lodges held fairly close ties with the professional organizations from which they had sprung or been derived. The first Grand Lodge of England was founded in 1717, at a time when the club was the favourite meeting-ground for Londoners. This obvious need of the Englishman to associate with his fellows, at the beginning of the eighteenth century in particular, appears to have been in part responsible for the development of both clubs and lodges. Twelve years before the accession of George III, a powerful rival lodge, calling itself the Ancients' Lodge, was founded. It referred to its rivals as the 'Moderns'. This rift was to endure until 1813, at which date the United Grand Lodge of England was formed.

There is no place here for the history of English freemasonry between the years 1760–1810. Instead we may point out a few of the features of life in a Freemason's Lodge at this time.

SOME FEATURES OF A FREEMASON'S LODGE

St George's Lodge at Taunton in Somerset was in existence from 1764 to 1783. The ceremonial opening of the Lodge was marked by a grand procession made up of the 'principal personages' of the town. The correspondent of the newspaper *St James's Chronicle*, describing the procession, remarks upon the 'genteel' appearance of its members, who wore aprons of white leather and gloves of the same colour with a mason's tools in silver hung about the neck. The correspondent was particularly impressed with the 'Tyler', his hat under his arm, naked sword in hand, followed by two stewards with their white rods of office. In pairs the procession moved up to the Fountain Tavern, where an 'elegant' dinner party was held. This Lodge was composed of members drawn from a high level of society; a fact confirmed by the official record for August 1, 1764. Of six new apprentices one was a colonel, one a gentleman, two were 'esquires', a fifth was a Doctor of Theology, while only one was a tradesman—a wine-merchant. This rather special example does not alter the fact that a great many lodges were composed of artisans, industrialists, shop-keepers, and non-commissioned officers. On December 27 St George's Lodge, along with the rest, celebrated the feast of St John the Evangelist: the brothers took part in a religious service during which they listened to a sermon on the text 'Love one another with brotherly love'. Bells rang as they walked out of church and they made their way still in procession to the Fountain Tavern to dine. In the afternoon the Lodge met again and the day ended, according to one brother, 'in the greatest harmony, pleasure and decorum'. The Lodge had its own assistance fund, but it also contributed to the general charitable fund of the Grand Lodge. In the course of time three of the brethren were elected to Parliament. From time to time the Lodge bought a few lottery tickets in the same way as other 'lottery clubs'. Meetings usually took place twice a month: the initiate paid an entry fee of two guineas, but as in the 'drinking clubs' a shilling to cover the cost of drinks was also payable upon each occasion. These details serve to explain the similarities between clubs and lodges. The real peculiarity of the lodges lay in the special rites performed at their meetings. Nor should we forget the magnificent ritual costumes worn by the members of certain clubs. Thus the members of Bucks' Lodge were fitted out with ornamental splendour, and were accepted into the Lodge according to the strictest of rules, the president being raised three feet above the other members. This was also true of the 'Sublime Society of the Beefsteaks', whose members, twenty-four in all, wore scarlet cloaks and blue jackets and waistcoats of chamois leather.

LIBERTINES AND BONS VIVANTS

This picture of English life would be incomplete without some mention of those various societies, often irreligious, where a point was sometimes made of parodying the most sacred ceremonies. These societies, which substituted the cult of the Devil for the worship of Our Lord, were generally known as the 'Hell-Fire Clubs'. In most cases it was difficult to distinguish masquerade and parody from sacrilegious intent; and since our knowledge of these semi-secret organizations comes to us only in the form of rumour, more or less ill-informed hearsay, and the charges levelled by opponents, it is scanty indeed.

The most famous of these clubs, however, was 'The Brotherhood of the Friars of St Francis', named in honour of its founder Sir Francis Dashwood, Lord le Despenser, Premier Baronet of England. For a short time Chancellor of the Exchequer, he was a friend of Benjamin Franklin and political figures of importance like the Earl of Sandwich, First Lord of the Admiralty (and inventor, furthermore, of the 'sandwich' which enabled him to dine without pausing while playing cards), Bubb Doddington (the future Lord Melcombe), Henry Vansittart, Governor of Bengal, the demagogue John Wilkes and the poet Churchill: even the incorrruptible magistrate Sir John D'Aubrey was a member. The date of foundation and the cessation of the society are not known; what is known is that in 1755 Dashwood rented the ruined Abbey of Medmenham and here the 'Franciscans' set up their headquarters. The last mention of it occurs in 1776, and then its meetings were no longer held at Medmenham, but in the famous caves at West Wycombe, home of Sir Francis Dashwood—though sometimes the 'friars' would meet at Eyethorpe, home of Sir William Stanhope, brother of Lord Chesterfield. The motto of the order was taken from Rabelais: '*Fay ce que Voudras*'. Women were, of course, admitted to the Abbey: local girls or professionals brought down from London by the scions of great houses. Sometimes there were even women of high society arriving masked, and consenting to show their faces only when convinced that there would be no dangerous encounters. The inscriptions and erotic statues which adorned the gardens and the buildings were not peculiar to Medmenham, for oddities of the kind could be seen on other estates. If we are to believe one contemporary newspaper report, no indelicate or indecent behaviour was allowed to pass unpunished: the forms of decorum and correctness had at all times to be observed (a similarity is here—on paper at least—with the freemasons). Two permanent dignitaries—the Superior and the Steward directed the order in the same manner as the Lodge. Each member took it in turns to play the role of Lord Abbot, wearing a red hat like a cardinal's. There is no certain proof that Black Masses were celebrated, as was alleged by enemies: on the other hand there was undoubtedly an enormous amount of gambling and drinking, as there was, for that matter, in every other club and elsewhere at this period.

Nor is much known about the Society of Demoniacs founded in Yorkshire by the squire John Hall-Stevenson. The Reverend Lawrence Sterne, a friend of the founder, was presumably also a member. The Demoniacs met at Skelton Castle, otherwise known as 'Crazy Castle'. Each member was known by a pseudonym: Hall-Stevenson was 'Antoine', another member 'The Cardinal' and so on. The library contained a fine collection of erotica which was turned to good account by Sterne in his work. Little more is known of the Demoniacs' activities.

The Sublime Society of the Beefsteaks in London, however, held no such dark mysteries: it was a club where members sought the good life, meeting in a room belonging to Covent Garden theatre. It was founded in 1735 by John Rich, director of the theatre. After the fire in Covent Garden in 1808 it continued to meet in Bedford Coffee-house, and later at the Lyceum Theatre. Most of the 'Franciscans' of Medmenham were members of this club as well: William Hogarth was a member and also a freemason; and in all probability he was admitted to Medmenham too. Given the number of clubs to which Englishmen belong today, it is clear that club life is an essential need—one of the permanent features of the national character.

The menu was invariably beefsteak, only the vegetable varied. The emblem of the Society was a grid-iron; its list of membership shows its close links with the theatre: names like Theophilus Cibber (the son of the author-director Colley Cibber) along with playwrights like Aaron Hill, George Colman, Arthur Murphy, etc., as well as actors like David Garrick and John Kemble. Many of the great, the Prince of Wales and the Duke of York among them, also belonged. The Beefsteak declined slowly through the reign of Queen Victoria, to disappear finally in 1869.

PART SIX

ENGLISH LIFE AND ITS CONTRASTS

CHAPTER ONE

THE MELANCHOLY OF MODERN ENGLAND

Seen as a whole the standard of living under George III showed a definite improvement—a fact indicated by the consumption of certain products regarded as luxury goods. Thus, the consumption of sugar rose from eight pounds per capita in 1760 to more than eighteen pounds in 1810. This increase, however, was not evenly distributed, since for many people sugar, like some other foodstuffs, was still a luxury article. The difference between the diet of rich and poor was still as marked as ever it had been in the past; possibly even more so. Yet the English seem to have been far more struck by the variation of living standards on the Continent than by the glaring anomalies of life among their own countrymen. Most of them felt like Doctor Johnson when he said: 'The great in France live very magnificently, but the rest very miserably. . . . The shops of Paris are mean; the meat in the markets is such as would be sent to a gaol in England.' At much the same time (in 1775) the Irish parson, Thomas Campbell, could observe: 'The people of France do not reflect that image of happiness which the English nation does in every quarter.' And, in the following year these words were confirmed by Johnson himself: '. . . there was no happy middle station as in England'. Campbell went so far as to declare that there was in England still a 'plethora' of meat and money. Before we condemn these two witnesses for exaggeration we must remember that they were both in fact comparing the middle classes of London and Paris rather than the masses. Thus limited, their judgments are to a great extent confirmed by Grosley: the London artisans earned double the wage of their equivalents in Paris: they 'eat and drink well, are handsomely clothed, and procreate accordingly'. It was true that life was 'so dear in London that tradesmen of the lower sort, though they earn a great deal, and are at no expense but what is unavoidable, and to procure bare necessaries live, as such people do everywhere else, from hand to mouth'. True in 1765 at least. But it seems that from 1790 onwards the living

173

standards of the working-class man and the peasant, as well as of the artisan, tended to fall, despite high wages, while the rich lived at an ever higher rate. In 1807 Southey made sport of the 'common people' and their pride in 'the roast-beef of Old England' at a time when in fact they had to content themselves with 'bread and potatoes'. The contrast between the leisured classes and the populace was extremely marked.

On December 19, 1795, Parson Woodforde was writing in his diary: 'Wheat very dear indeed . . . wheat flour very difficult to get at all'; yet some days earlier he had given a dinner to twenty-one farmers from Weston Longeville—a meal which consisted of 'three joints of beef, a leg of mutton, of fish, rabbits, plenty of puddings, of both small and strong beer, punch (made from six bottles of rum), of wine, and five bottles of port'. Some weeks later he received five of his friends to dinner, and regaled them with ham, a couple of chickens, a saddle of mutton, a cod, a duck, cauliflowers, potatoes, cucumbers, macaroni, a pudding, jellies, oranges, almonds, raisins, walnuts, etc., with port, sherry, beer, coffee and tea to drink. 'My guests,' Woodforde observed, 'appeared to have had enough.'

These contrasts in the living standards between rich and poor could not help but create the sort of conditions in which social unrest would flourish: in Nottingham, for instance, the latter years of the century were overshadowed by popular unrest, mainly caused by the famine and the high cost of living. In 1792 a crowd of men and women protested against the high price of meat by tearing down doors and windows in the butchers' shops and piling them on to an enormous bonfire in the streets. In 1796, and again in 1797, starving mobs sacked the bakeries; while twice in 1800 the shortage of bread set off violent rioting. It was during the years between 1796–1800 that a peak of unrest was reached in Nottingham and in the country as a whole.

But in fact life for the past twenty years had been growing progressively more difficult for the labouring classes. The optimistic views expressed by Grosley were not inaccurate at the time of his visit to England, but this was to be the last of the years of relatively cheap living. From 1765 the high cost of food was to be a source of constant difficulty to the authorities: in 1766 in Glasgow and Edinburgh the export of a number of products was forbidden. From 1770 in London and Bristol societies were formed aimed at 'reducing the exorbitant prices of butchers' meat'. In 1766 after

174

outbreaks of trouble at Reading, Newark, Gloucester and Salisbury, a special commission set up to pronounce judgment on the 'rioters' sentenced twenty-eight of the accused to death, five to deportation and fifteen to prison: this was the year of the notorious 'cheese riots' in Nottingham, when cheeses were used as brickbats: one of them hit the Lord Mayor while he was reading the Riot Acts. He fell unconscious and had to be carried into the Exchange.

Boswell in London in 1775 was talking to a waterman as he rowed him up the Thames: 'The waterman complained of the high price of provisions, and said if a poor man could live now he might live for ever.' And Boswell adds a comment: 'This was a curious expression that provisions never would be dearer.' Unfortunately the waterman was wrong; foodstuffs as we have seen, were to reach even higher prices twenty years later.

And yet there was one economic feature common to each and every class in the reign of George III—the matter of personal debts.

DEBTS

The multiplicity if not the universality of debtors is astonishing. In the reign of George III the poor pawned their tools, their clothes, their furniture (or their landlord's), for food and drink. The pawnbroker was essential to daily life: the three golden balls hanging outside his shop could be seen on every side. A pamphlet published in 1809 denounced usury as practised by those demanding interest at 100 per cent or more, although since 1800 the maximum rate that could legally be charged was 20 per cent. The magistrate Colquhoun in 1806 declared that some were lending at interest rates as high as 3,000 per cent. When a pauper no longer had anything to pawn, he would steal. When arrested he was forced to borrow again in order to pay the gaoler's fees. Many had to stay in prison once their sentence had been served, simply because they lacked the means to discharge themselves. The rich ran into debt as often as the poor, though not for the same reasons: gaming was the most usual cause, and when there was no more money to pay one's losses, one pledged one's sword, one's watch, one's jewellery. But for the rich there were less frivolous reasons than gambling for running into debt. A great landowner inheriting a family estate had to provide a dowry for his sister when she married, or, if she never married, a pension—which sometimes provided for younger brothers as well. But there was rarely the means to pay out money on this scale, and this meant further borrowing. Sometimes too the heir wished to round off his estates, and to acquire the land he needed had to borrow again: Boswell himself acquired a property of this sort, and nine years later he still owed his father £1,300.

It was not only young bloods like Charles James Fox who fell into debt: his political opponent, William Pitt, despite a fund which was opened on his behalf, the accumulation of sinecures and the bankers who came to his rescue, still died leaving £40,000 worth of debts which in his case were certainly not incurred as a result of debauchery or gambling. Among the 'serious' causes of running into debt were the expenses incurred in maintaining a seat in Parliament, which was frequently obligatory for those possessing large estates, or because of the family tradition or local custom, quite apart from any personal ambition. In general the great land-owner was expected to live on a certain scale, to run a large household whose members were accustomed to help themselves to his belongings. Thus, in 1775, when Lord Pembroke was not in residence at Wilton House, he still spent £100 a month to keep fires going in the rooms—a small example of the sort of 'leakage' which was perfectly usual at this level; indeed, only a very insignificant example when one thinks of the fortunes, often very considerable, which superior servants (men of business, lawyers, and agents) ran up on behalf of their master or their clients. William Beckford of Fonthill, for instance, borrowed money from his own agents to make up the deficiencies in his income which they themselves had caused.

When things became really too difficult the Englishman would go off to live abroad, not only because in this way he put the Channel between himself and his creditors, but also because the cost of living in France and Italy was considerably less. A friend of the Reverend William Cole, a Captain Reddall, went out to live at Saint-Omer, at the house of Madame Descamps, 'opposite the Belle Croix', where for £18 a year he could obtain full board and lodging. But sometimes the well-born debtor went farther to escape his creditors—setting forth on the final journey into the hereafter, like John Damer, when his father Lord Milton, refused to pay his debts.

13. Fishmonger and Milkmaid (Rowlandson)

14. Execution at Newgate (Rowlandson)

If a young man in middle-class circumstances attempted to emulate the sort of life the aristocracy led he inevitably fell into debt, and when his parents grew tired of paying his debts they sent him, as the lawyer William Hickey was sent, to India, or taking advantage of any influential relations they might possess, had him sent to sea as a midshipman. If all else failed there was nothing for it but prison—either Marshalsea or the Fleet—unless the debtor could find a friend to stand bail for him, while he himself escaped. Even then, the guarantor himself risked prison if he could not pay.

However extraordinary it may seem, debts at this period were a part even of middle-class existence. Edmund Burke the Irish parvenu, whose family were loath to part with money, managed to surmount his financial crises only thanks to his friends, and to the benevolence of Lord Rockingham, who wiped out in his will a debt of some £30,000. Even when individual debts did not amount to this sort of figure the debtor considered it quite normal to be importuned by his creditors, so normal indeed that an expression coined in the seventeenth century became current in the eighteenth to describe this sort of harassment: to be 'dunned', from the word 'dun' meaning an importunate creditor. Thus Parson Woodforde, a serious enough character economical, and anyhow very comfortable off, received 'dunning' letters from his wine merchant or demands from his tailor, which did not seem to perturb him very much: in every social class debts were a part of the eighteenth-century way of life, as much perhaps even more, than credit is today.

GAMING AND BETTING

Although not all fell into debt yet almost all spent a considerable part of leisure in gaming: in clubs, coffee-houses, the drawing-rooms of the aristocracy, middle-class households, low-class taverns, there were card parties everywhere (faro, basset, quadrille, whist and so on). There was dishonour neither in being ruined at cards, nor in winning a fortune. Thus in 1755 John Scott, an army captain, had nothing but a few debts to his name; by 1774 his fortune was estimated at half a million pounds. This rapid rise to fortune was accomplished entirely at the card-tables. Scott entered Parliament and his three daughters were to become Duchess of Portland, Lady Doune and Viscountess Canning.

Wagering, like card-playing, was by no means confined to the upper classes. Everyone laid bets on everything: the result of a horse-race, a cock-fight, a boxing-match, or a wrestling match, on an election, on how many years the Duke of this or that might live; on a throw of dice, on a game of darts or bowls, on the sex of an unborn child, on the accuracy of some quotation. Parson Wood-forde often laid bets of from 6d to 2 or 3 shillings, on the chances of rain falling before morning, or of frost on a particular date, or the result of a set of tennis. In 1767 Boswell gave supper to two friends with whom he had wagered a guinea he would not contract a venereal disease for three years. He lost the bet of course, and what is more that very evening when supper was over he visited a house of ill-fame where he contracted a new infection. The State seemed virtually to encourage gaming; between 1694 and 1784 forty-two official lotteries were held in succession, with winning tickets in a proportion of one to five. Private lotteries were for-bidden. But methods of insurance against loss were really lotteries in themselves. After 1793 when they were forbidden they were held in secret. If private lotteries were illegal in principle they could always be authorized by special decision of Parliament. Was not life itself in this century a great game of chance, a veritable lottery? Had not the Book of Ecclesiastes said, and the preachers were end-lessly reiterating it, 'the race is not to the swift, nor the battle to the strong, neither yet bread to the wise, nor yet riches to men of under-standing, nor yet favour to men of skill, but time and chance happeneth to them all'.

But while eighteenth-century England was the country par excellence for gaming, it was also the country of insurance. In 1765 Grosley marvelled at the way both houses and their contents in London were insured against fire: 'these expedients . . . have not yet been made use of at Paris'. In fact an even more im-portant innovation had already been made: James Dodson the mathematician had in 1762 invented a form of *scientific* life-insurance (ordinary life-insurance had been in existence a long time past). George III's reign was in every way a period of signi-ficant development in scientific techniques which amounted to a craze. We saw earlier how this fashion gave birth to numerous societies, even infiltrating into private life, when men like Lackington introduced scientific discussions into their own homes.

But, if the eighteenth century was the century of science and reason, it was also a century of error, superstition and charlatanism.

ERROR, SUPERSTITION AND CHARLATANISM

In the autumn of 1768 Doctor Johnson explained gravely to Boswell how, at the approach of winter, swallows cling together in a ball, or 'conglobulate', sleeping through winter at the bottom of the rivers. When it thundered at night, the whole of Parson Woodforde's household would rise from their beds, and hurl themselves shrieking against the parson's door: this was in 1787, more than thirty-six years after Franklin's observations on electricity and thunder had been published in England. On his way to Norwich one morning Woodforde went to look at the 'wise pig' and on the same evening attended 'an excellent conference on astronomy'. Furthermore, whenever some 'curiosity' came to Norwich—a dwarf maybe or a girl without arms—the vicar of Weston Longeville would invariably make a special journey to see it.

Parson Woodforde attached great importance to dreams. When in a dream one night he saw Jenny Woodforde clothed in white, pale but very lovely, he prayed that the apparition did not presage some evil to her kin. When, however, he dreamed that he had lost his hat at a banquet and awaking next morning spied a rook flying over the parsonage he had no longer any doubt: these were signs of misfortune. Yet when his brother John felt himself being followed by a light while crossing a field Woodforde was not so sure: it could perhaps have been a mere reflection in the snow-covered field, rather than a presentiment of death. He was torn between these two interpretations. He was uncertain and the whole century with him.

Indeed this era of progress in the field of science was one in which the charlatan grew rich: the German Bossy who harangued the crowd at Covent Garden; the Italian Dominecetti who ran a Turkish bath establishment in Chelsea; Doctor Marmeduke, who practised animal magnetism in Bloomsbury (following Mesmer and de Loutherbourg). Perhaps the most famous of all was Doctor Graham, whose 'Temple of Health', established in a house in Adelphi Terrace, proposed to cure barren women and impotent men by means of a 'balsam' dispensed for a guinea a bottle. If this did not succeed in curing the infirmity, then one could fall back on one of those 'magneto-electric' beds, where a couple could lie for £50 a night. And finally if for some outlandish reason this cure also failed, then a night could be spent in the voluptuous 'celestial bed' which at £100 was even more expensive, but would certainly prove infallible.

Nevertheless during the reign of George III medicine made some progress.

DISEASE AND MEDICINE

From 1796 vaccination (invented by Jenner) began slowly to replace inoculation, sometimes effectively, and at least less dangerously. Smallpox apart, the two main groups of illness at this period were still 'fevers' or 'ague', and venereal diseases. The Scotsman William Cullen put his finger on the two main causes of 'fever': contagions and miasmas emanating from marshy ground. But these conclusions did not help much in practice, and when it became necessary to prescribe some remedy, bleeding still held the place of honour.

In any case the poor had no money to pay the doctor, while better off families were quite happy to consult a compendium of prescriptions: for example, John Quincy's *English Pharmacopeia*, which reached its fourteenth, but by no means its last edition in 1769. Even more popular was a little book by none other than John Wesley: *Primitive Physic—or an Easy and Natural Method of Curing Most Diseases*. This work reached its twenty-sixth edition in 1805, and was reprinted in the Victorian era. There were a dozen remedies against cancer such as: 'Take a mellow apple, cut off the top, take out the core, fill the hole with hogs' grease; then cover it with the top and roast the apple thoroughly. Take off the paring, beat the pap well, spread it thick on linen, and lay it warm on the sore, putting a bladder over it. Change this every twelve or twenty-four hours.' And, again according to Wesley, certain cancers were cured by daily bathing in cold water and the drinking of water.

Mercury was the traditional cure for venereal diseases, but Keyser's pills received a great deal of publicity in the press; they cured scurvy, leprosy, tumours, stiffness of the joints, gout and rheumatism as well. In fact gout was becoming the disease of the leisured classes; it was caused both by a rising standard of living and by the lack of physical exercise. Venereal diseases were also

180

treated by Doctor Kennedy's powder and the 'Lisbon Diet Drink' of which we spoke on page 125. But the queen of panaceas was certainly Doctor James's powder, sovereign against 'fevers, small-pox, measles, pleurisy, quinsy, acute rheumatism, colds, every inflammatory and epidemic illness, as well as nervous disease, hypo-chondria and hysterics'. All in all there was a cure for every disease except death itself.

DEATH

While money preserved no one from death, it usually governed the magnitude of the tribute accorded to those whom it claimed. M. Grosley in 1765 was amazed at the cost of dying! Burial in a church was only for the very rich; the digging of a grave even in a cemetery cost as much as a guinea: 'a bill which I was shown of the expenses for burying in a churchyard a child of one of the lower sort of people, aged three years, amounted to two guineas'. This was a feature of eighteenth-century life which the French could not easily reconcile with their notion of an ideal England—demo-cratic, egalitarian. Somewhat later another traveller was writing: 'In France, the expenses of the funeral train, the dress and other magnificence may ruin a family. At a burying in London half an inheritance may be expended.'

But epitaphs were carved on every gravestone, middle and upper class alike. Elegiac verse was a common literary form throughout the eighteenth century. Practised by Pope, Johnson and many others, it was most highly developed in the time of George III. Famous anthologies were published, notably by Frobisher and, especially after his conversion to Evangelism, James Lackington. Amateurs like Mrs Thrale or Parson Woodforde, for instance, could rhyme an epitaph on the death of a relation, a friend or neighbour with great nicety; and Francis Grose, the celebrated wit, collected from the graveyards any lines that amused him, adding to them compositions of his own.

The shops of the funeral undertakers in London and other great cities astonished foreign travellers with their splendour:

'Very fine shops elegantly filled with coffins of every kind and colour, ornamented with deaths' heads, crossed bones and other gloomy motives displayed like precious jewels to satisfy every variety of vanity. Shops of this kind are lighted up at night, like our own jewellers and dress shops, to tempt the passer-by who may come to contemplate his own funeral in advance, or is perhaps already tired of life.'

The notion that the English were attracted by the thought of death was often expressed by foreign visitors: 'The concern shown by the English over the manner of their burial makes one think that they take more pleasure in dying than in living,' and visitors from France felt that they had found an explanation of the 'spleen' or melancholy, the 'English disease', as foreigners called it.

THE 'ENGLISH DISEASE'

Most Frenchmen were mystified by this national characteristic: Why, demands M. Grosley, this melancholy 'in every family, in circles, in assemblies, at public and private entertainments'? Why do such crowds go to Ranelagh, to Vauxhall, and other pleasure spots, since 'the joy which they seem in search of at these places does not beam through their countenances; they look as grave at Vauxhall as at the Bank, at church, or a private club'. Why did the English peasant, 'well-fed, well-lodged and at his ease', have 'as serious and melancholy an air'? While the peasant in France, 'persecuted and harassed by thousands', impoverished, often starving, seemed nevertheless gay, dancing and singing at every turn, just as Smollett, and later Sterne in his *Sentimental Journey* describe him?

The explanations offered by contemporaries are various and improbable; they attribute it for instance to the beer (but what about the village fairs in Flanders?); or to the coal (but what of the miners in the north of France?); to the rain then (but what about Normandy?). Besides, these explanations were often contradictory: one of them attributed the English gloom to the 'satiety' born of too much wealth, another to the poverty resulting from the 'high price of victuals'. The one blamed English 'incontinency', the other puritanism. The longing for 'respectability' does not date from the Victorians, and maybe at the time of George III more and more classes of society were aspiring to a 'serious' attitude which was not conducive to gaiety. 'In England,' observed Boswell to Rousseau, 'they are stiff and silent, in order to win respect.' Nowadays the reasons for the English disease are examined at deeper levels: the theory is advanced that tensions were created by the conflict arising between scientific discovery and religious dogma. But apart from the fact that this cause could affect only a tiny proportion of the population, the same tensions existed in France as in England, and thinking people there do not seem to have suffered from this 'disease'.

The truth is that 'the English disease' was not a sickness of the individual, but a collective illness which grew from deeper roots: the development of manufacturing, perhaps, the division of labour, the heavy industries which served to break up rural communities, the disruption of family and social ties contributed too, together with the disappearance of a traditional culture along with its festivals, its dance and song; man was rapidly alienated from man.

What observers failed to discern, since 'Old and Merrie England' was not suddenly extinguished, was the magnitude of all this change.

CHAPTER TWO

JOHN BULL'S MERRYMAKING

While the influence of Evangelism during this period was gradually to improve standards of behaviour, the effects, like those of the Industrial Revolution, were not immediately discernible. From the earliest years of this reign, if Boswell's behaviour was influenced by the outward appearance of 'gravity' in manners and conversation, this was only because qualities of the kind were becoming more and more indispensable to worldly success. But the same Boswell, like many of his contemporaries, considered that 'fornication' was not a 'heinous sin', only that it was imprudent to indulge it unless a young and healthy girl presented an 'extraordinary' opportunity. And his friend the Reverend Robert Richardson, almoner to Sir Joseph Yorke, was in no way shocked when the usual custom of his parish was observed and 'the young fellows got the girls with child first, without any idea of harm, and then married them'. He said, Boswell tells us, 'this showed what couples loved each other, and he never blamed them'. The Reverend William Cole—very High Church—had to be, perhaps, less tolerant. Yet between 1765 and 1767, of the couples marrying in his parish many of the girls were already pregnant, and he does not appear to have been unduly shocked. It sometimes happened that offspring would arrive on the day of their parents' wedding; but Cole seemed in no way upset; he baptised the children and then married their parents.

Forty years later scandals of this sort would come to be denounced with indignation by the Evangelicals and by Churchmen of every denomination. The *Memoirs* of a gentleman's valet, Macdonald, are equally illustrative of developments in behaviour between the beginning and the end of the reign. When in 1762 Major Joass took over command of the garrison in Stirling, his first care was to appoint one soldier to assist Macdonald and another to polish his table knives. Then he organized a ball and supper in

184

honour of the ladies and gentlemen of the county. The morning after the ball he questioned his servant:

'John, which of those ladies did you fall for?'

'Miss Fairly, Sir.'

'I'm hanged if I wouldn't have chosen the very same!' And, Macdonald remarked: 'The Major laughed heartily, for he was a cheerful man and did not care to stand on ceremony.' 'Free and merry'—and the spirit of Old England was abroad not only in the soldiery, but also in the men of law.

Some of these, after a trial held in 1776, went off to fortify themselves on beefsteak, and during dinner, says Boswell, 'the three lawyers made up songs for a "Criminal Opera" . . . as for instance "We're not guilty yet" to the tune of "We're gayly yet". Such ludicrous extravagances diverted us extremely. We laughed and sung and drank Claret till past eleven at night.'

'Free and Merry' too were the English, even in the Upper House. 'I have heard Lords Lyttleton, Temple, Pomfret and the old Duke of Newcastle speak: the latter delivered himself, as he was leaning on two young lords, who sat before him upon the second bench. . . . In the midst of a warm debate the Lord Chancellor rose, made a long and vehement harangue, and terminated his discourse by a stroke which set the whole house a-laughing.' And, finishes Grosley: 'Who would not, upon seeing the greatest personages of England treating the most important State affairs in this manner . . . be tempted to look upon the English as the gayest, most jovial, and the most addicted to buffoonery of all nations?' And the Duke of Newcastle was seventy-two at the time! These aristocrats were also free in their speech, and did not stand on ceremony. When James Ogilvy, sixth Earl of Findlater, introduced one of his natural sons he did so without a trace of embarrassment: 'This is my bastard!' Even Boswell thought this peculiar. Only fifteen years earlier Beckford, then Lord Mayor, would speak with pride of his numerous bastards, and occasion no surprise; but by 1764 Lord Findlater was looked upon as somewhat eccentric.

Any 'free and merry' aspects of England at this period are readily seen in the marvellous water-colours and drawings of Thomas Rowlandson. But in these works there is another side to the 'freedom'—their lively-looking faces and their unrestrained emotions expressed so freely are clearly confirmed in memoirs of contemporary writers.

185

When Boswell returned to London from a journey to Europe, he 'embraced' his friend Temple in the 'old' manner: that is to say he pressed him against his heart, and the following day it was Johnson who grasped him in his turn, seizing him by the waist like a sack of coals. Two years later, says Boswell, when Johnson met him on his return to London from Edinburgh 'he took me in his arms and kissed me on both cheeks'. Jacques Meister in 1790 wrote that 'the kiss of love and the kiss of friendship are impressed alike on the lips'. No one attempted to conceal emotion: people cried openly at tragedy and laughed heartily at farce. The father of the young Hickey was certainly no sentimentalist, since he was public prosecutor in Chancery Lane; yet when he was told the good opinion that Hickey's employer had of the boy (who had lately been in trouble), he burst into tears, held him to his heart and kissed him on the cheek.

Since every man from Lord Nelson to William Hickey felt free to display his emotions, it is clear that Doctor Arnold the educationalist and his followers had not yet laid down the 'stiff upper lip' as the distinctive mark of the 'gentleman'. Not that the eighteenth-century man was in any way effeminate. Far from it— he cultivated manliness and practised it from early childhood: any visitor from abroad could vouch for that.

THE CULTIVATION OF MANLINESS

M. Grosley, remarking upon 'the faces . . . generally very handsome and with the air of the utmost mildness' of the pupils of Westminster and Eton, observed that 'they are the most intractable and the most obstinate creatures that ever came out of the hands of nature. . . . To make up for this, they are mad for violent exercises, the want of which they already feel.' The taste for boxing was universal, not only among men, but women as well 'at least among the populace'. M. Grosley continues with an example of this fighting spirit which would seem to have been devised with Rowlandson's paintbrush in mind:

'In Holborn I saw a woman engaged with a man, who, taking all sorts of advantages, flew at her with a rage of which the most frightful symptoms could be seen in his attitude and in all the features of his face: having struck her with the utmost force, he

186

retreated and, pouring out torrents of abuse, he returned again to the attack. The woman, who appeared less furious than he, seized these intervals to fall upon his face and eyes with her hands. I saw five or six bouts of the combat, which surprised me very much since the woman had upon her left arm an infant a year or two old, which, far from crying out, as it is natural for children to do, did not so much as seem to knit its brow, but appeared to attend to the lesson of what it was one day to practise itself.'

There are other descriptions of the same sort as a prelude to the pictures which Rowlandson painted. Grosley's descriptions are less violent but equally evocative. Thus, when he went down to Eton, and stepped into a draper's shop to await his friends: 'During the short stay we made there, about a dozen of the scholars came to buy biscuits, sugar-plums and other sweetmeats. There was a buxom wench belonging to the shop, whom some of the young gentlemen caressed and kissed in front of us.' Grosley does not, however, mention that these 'diversions' were a part, like boxing, of the English conception of manliness. It was no accident that venereal diseases were at this period known as 'manly diseases'.

The subjects of George III cultivated the virtues of 'manliness' as well as its vices. The monarch himself gave an example of manly virtue. When he was eighteen the future George III was writing: 'I will take upon me the man in everything.' And again the following year: 'I am resolved in myself . . . to act the man in everything.' A few years later Boswell was to write in his journal: 'Indulge not whims but form into a man.' And his advice included: 'Above all things a young man should guard against effeminacy. I would advise him to avoid warm baths and accustom himself rather to the cold bath, which will give him vigour and liveliness.' His advice to himself: 'At all events be manly.' And the reason he admired John Wilkes, whose agnosticism and political opinions he did not share, was because he looked upon this demagogue as the personi-fication of masculinity: 'I do admire your strength of mind, and look upon you as one of the vigorous few who keep up the true manly character in this effeminate age.'

In this Boswell was echoing the contemporary English moralist, who was convinced that England was a decadent country, and who was obsessed by the fear of contemplating a nation becoming irredeemably effeminate. It may be that the image of John Bull

187

might not have assumed such meaning in eighteenth-century England, had the English not wished so devoutly to preserve themselves in their own eyes from this effeminacy, which they looked upon as a national threat.

A real threat did exist, however, and this was that the fear of being or of seeming effeminate, could lead to the acceptance of brutality or downright cruelty.

CRUELTY, BEASTLINESS, HUMANITY

The most popular sports of the reign were bloodsports: dogs for chasing duck over water, for baiting badgers, bulls and so on, were specially bred for the purpose. Cockfighting in specially designed pits took place not only in London, but also between villages and counties: one fight between the champions of Somerset and Wiltshire went on for two days; sometimes as many as sixteen cocks on each side fought until the whole side was wiped out, after which the winning team was divided into two, and the fight continued until such time as one bird only remained alive. The game of cockthrowing was crueller still—sticks were thrown at a tethered cockerel, and the game went on until the bird died.

The treatment meted out to children was no better. When young Macdonald was working as postilion, the coachman, suspecting that the child was keeping a proportion of the tips for himself, beat his legs until the blood flowed. When the Reverend William Cole's young servant was overlong in returning from an errand, the clergyman struck him with a bludgeon, and when he was drunk had him whipped; Doctor Pettigal, a parson and a distinguished member of the Archaeological Society, kicked his maidservant, according to Cole 'very severely', when she did not run fast enough to do his bidding. And when the girl dared to complain of her master, the local justice was 'honest' enough to declare her complaint invalid —as a 'courteous gesture on behalf of a neighbour'. Doctor Pettigal, according to another of his friends, was right to do so since she was not a good servant.

There was collective as well as individual violence: when the populace had something to celebrate, it would insist that all the windows of the town be lit up, and any that were not were broken. When the mob was in an angry mood, it broke windows that were lit as well as those that were not. It was the custom—a custom well documented in a letter addressed in 1769 by Lord Hailes to Boswell after the mob had celebrated in its customary manner the lawyer's success in the Douglas Affair: 'Had the mob satisfied themselves with breaking my windows and throwing stones which might have murdered the family, I might have been less displeased when the first attack was over. But renewed attacks not at windows but at my door, in order to break it open, *these* are insults which every man of spirit and dignity must feel. . . .'

Human life itself was of little account—unless, of course, the subject was a gentleman. Johnson remarked of the American colonists in revolt: 'They are a race of convicts and ought to be thankful for anything we allow them short of hanging.' Furthermore, until 1783, a hanging at Tyburn (now Marble Arch) was one of the gladdest occasions in the London calendar.

The depths of beastliness and brutality, not only among the lower orders but in the solid middle class itself, are unimaginable. Hogarth's picture of the traditional Lord Mayor's Banquet in London is well known. Of course the guests are sodden with drink and food, but the scene seems positively honeyed in comparison with the description of a similar banquet in 1780 by an actual witness, at a period when habits were no longer quite as brutish as in Hogarth's time:

'In five minutes after the guests took their stations at the tables, the dishes were entirely cleared of their contents, twenty hands seizing the same joint of a bird and literally tearing it to pieces. A more determined scramble could not be, the roaring and noise was deafening and hideous, which increased as the liquor operated, bottles and glasses flying across from side to side, without intermission. Such a bear garden altogether I never beheld, except my first visit to Wetherby's, which it brought very forcibly to my recollection.'

When we consider that those taking part were all by definition ratepayers and people of substance, we have some measure of the beastliness and brutality of a middle class which the intellectuals had for more than half a century been attempting to civilize.

In a sense, however, the Establishment set the tone: throughout the reign and even after it the press-gang was the approved system of recruitment for the Navy in wartime. This consisted in rounding up and carrying off by force as required, any peaceful citizen from town or village who was unlucky enough to run into the press-gangers. In 1770 one of these gangs actually broke into a church in Southwark in south London while a marriage service was in progress and attempted to abduct the bridegroom; the surprise attack failed but in the confusion the clergyman was struck in the chest; the groom was lucky to escape, for until 1816 the law of Habeas Corpus had no legal application to victims of the press-gang.

The England of George III was a hard world in which the weak received no quarter. When young Humphry Clinker in Smollett's novel was sacked by the Marlborough innkeeper, who could not be bothered to care for him when he fell ill, Doctor Bramble treated him to a sarcastic tirade: 'Hark ye, Clinker, you are a most notorious offender. You stand convicted of sickness, hunger, wretchedness and want.' In 1770 the conception of social justice was clearly not so different from that of *Erewhon* in Samuel Butler's satirical Utopia.

Crimes against property were punished by most stringent measures: Boswell, as a young lawyer, compromised his entire career because he defended too enthusiastically a client suspected of having stolen some sheep who was later condemned and hanged. The only appeal against the severity of the law was to the indulgence of the jury. The theft of a shilling incurred the death penalty. James Hardy Vaux was convicted for stealing a handkerchief: in the normal course of justice he would have been hanged, since the handkerchief according to the prosecution was worth 2s. However, the jury found that the handkerchief was worth only 11d and Vaux was condemned instead to seven years of forced labour in Australia. Eight years later he was convicted for stealing a ring from a shop, and condemned to death—a sentence which was later commuted to deportation. Larceny from a house was until 1832 still punishable by death—burglary likewise, until 1833. The crime of forgery led inevitably to death—a sentence from which there was no appeal whatsoever, even in the case of a clergyman such as Doctor Dodd, although Doctor Johnson intervened on his behalf, and the Queen herself put in a plea. Nor even when the culprit was a woman, as in 1809 the case of Margaret Barrington, who had falsely represented herself as the widow of a soldier, in order that she might draw on a portion of the deceased's estate. In the same way anyone

190

responsible for forging a signature could not hope for clemency: his crime was regarded as an offence against the entire financial system on which all business depended.

Yet what impressed Grosley and others was not the severity of the law but the humanity with which it was enforced, and the guarantees it afforded the accused: the granting of bail, the right of objection to some witness or other, and the demand for a public enquiry: 'Every circumstance,' says M. Grosley, 'tends to the acquittal of the prisoner, in conformity to the voice of nature which cries out: rather save twenty guilty persons, than put one innocent man to death'; this from a citizen of France, where the *'lettre de cachet'* was still the order of the day. It is true that this 'voice of nature' did not always echo that of the people.

One evening on his way to the British Museum M. Grosley found himself at the crossroads of Seven Dials, where 'the place was crowded with people waiting to see a poor wretch stand in the pillory whose punishment was deferred to another day. The mob, provoked at this disappointment, vented their rage on all that passed that way, whether a-foot or in coaches; and threw at them dirt, rotten eggs, dead dogs, and all sorts of trash and ordure which they had provided to pelt the unhappy wretch, according to custom.' On other occasions however, the mob knew exactly how to behave: 'At public festivals and all ceremonies which attract a crowd, let it be ever so great, children and persons low in stature, are seen to meet with tender treatment; all are eager to make room for them, and even to lift them up in their arms, that they have an opportunity of seeing.' There was seldom any need to restrain the mob by force: 'The passages and doors of the place where the festival is celebrated are guarded by persons who have no guns, partisans or halberds for their arms, but long hollow staves, which, when they make use of them, a case that happens very rarely, make a great noise, and do but little hurt.' And, as most visitors confirmed, it was not disagreeable to mingle with this sort of crowd, since most of the people in it were clean and well-dressed.

THE CLEANNESS OF ENGLAND

According to Pastor Moritz the English were remarkably clean and M. Grosley says the same of their houses. He seems to have been much impressed by the floorboards 'of excellent deal', which were 'washed and scrubbed almost daily' and had 'a whitish appearance and an air of freshness and cleanliness'. In this respect: 'the inhabitants of that city seem to vie with the Hollanders. The plate, hearthstones, movables, apartments, doors, stairs, the very street-doors, their locks and the large brass knockers are every day washed, scoured and rubbed.' In the Royal Hospital at Chelsea: 'the refectories of our richest Benedictine monks are hog-sties in comparison to that of this hospital', and at the Naval Hospital at Greenwich the cleanness was comparable 'to that of the cells of our nuns'.

That may be, but when Parson Woodforde travelled to London in 1786 and stayed at the Bell Savage Inn he was kept awake by fleas, and was finally driven to spending the night fully dressed in an arm-chair. In 1809 Matthew Gregory Lewis, the author of *The Monk* and a prosperous member of the middle class, wrote to his mother:

My dear Mother,
. . . With *real pain* I inform you, that the bugs and fleas are in compleat possession of your whole House, not excepting the Drawing-room; they have kept me awake for the two last nights; I have sent for the Bug-wash, but I fear, the attempt to get rid of them is a desperate one. . . .

Your affec^{te.} Son,
Matthew Gregory Lewis

There were cabinetmakers at this time who claimed to sell furniture certified free of vermin—an unlikely guarantee in view of the large number of tradesmen who called themselves 'bug destroyers'. Some of these professed themselves in their advertisements to have been granted a Royal warrant: *Bug-destroyer to His Majesty*. In 1775 a claim was made by one of these experts that he had rid more than 16,000 beds of vermin. But the eighteenth century, so proud of its improvements, yet does not seem to have found methods of dealing with vermin to improve on the conventional fumigation and burning.

THE LONGING FOR PROGRESS

In George III's reign 'improvement' was the one essential: if you rebuilt your house in the current fashion, then this was an 'improvement'. Publication of a new periodical was designed to 'improve' both the reader and the journalist. New agricultural procedures were introduced for the 'improvement' of the land. When, at the end of his university education one sent one's son to the Continent to do the Grand Tour, it was designed to 'improve' his education. As Johnson remarked: 'A man who has not been in Italy is always conscious of an inferiority from his not having seen what it is expected a man should see.' Foreign fashions predominated at the beginning of the reign, both in architecture and painting.

Yet already, despite the theories of Sir William Chambers and Sir Joshua Reynolds, James Wyatt and the Adam brothers were shaking off the yoke of the disciples of Palladio, while watercolourists like Alexander, John Robert Cozens, Francis Towne and others were the founders of an original and truly English school. What is more the middle classes in England were beginning to take an interest in their own island: Arthur Young's travels, and the work of Thomas Pennant, William Gilpin and John Byng all have much in common with the paintings of the English landscape painters, Gainsborough and Richard Wilson in particular. Soon the French Revolution and the Napoleonic Wars were to put an end to the 'Grand Tour' of the English, thereby impelling them to discover their own country, and rendering their nationalism, already fairly acute, yet more aggressive.

ENGLISH NATIONALISM

Hate and mistrust of the foreigner were not the prerogatives of the English alone, and even in England there was nothing new in feelings of the kind. According to prevailing circumstances, the Irish, Scots and Italians had all been subject to chauvinism. But under George III, and for clear historical reasons, France as commercial rival of England was singled out. Periodicals of the time emphasize the servile and effeminate character of the French. And while writers from France were full of adulation for the institutions of England, the English had nothing but contempt for those 'Popish' drinkers of thin soup, who were shod in wooden shoes. Johnson was of the same opinion as Smollett, and Smollett's views were shared by the populace; the conception of the Frenchman reflected in *Roderick Random* in 1748 did not change in any

N

way until the new century, or at least not until 1793, when he became a Jacobin regicide, feasting on blood. Indeed, as early as 1782, the Frenchman had already established his reputation for bloodthirsty ways according to the evidence of Pastor Moritz: Moritz was travelling in a stage-coach when tales of highwaymen were being told, and one of his fellow-travellers 'began to stand up for the honour of English highwaymen as opposed to his opposite number in France. The English, he said, robbed you, but the French robbed you and murdered you as well.' We may smile. But the unsavoury reputation of the French in England was to some extent understandable. The refugee Huguenots in England according to Grosley 'were all incessantly exclaiming against France', and broadcasting unfavourable impressions of the country. On the other hand they founded families, and carved illustrious names in sculpture (Roubiliac), in military prowess (Lord Ligonier), in the theatre (David Garrick), and in trade or industry (Molyneux). These examples did not alter the fact that the majority of them lived humbly in London and found work in spheres of employment where the standard of life was very low, notably among the silk-weavers of Spitalfields.

Another reason for the overweening francophobia was that throughout the whole of the eighteenth century there was a very real fear of French competition, especially in the silk industry, which, the English workman believed, could lead to his own unemployment. The French dancing masters employed by the aristocracy in England also helped to attach to their country of birth a reputation for frivolity and dandyism. And finally, London was not only the refuge of the Huguenots but also of bankrupts and of every kind of adventurer, which could be particularly harmful to the trade of the country. There were plenty of playwrights too, and these were unable to resist representing the Frenchman in a ridiculous or unpleasant light. However, we must remember that 'perfidious Gaul' from the previous century had had a counterpart in France—'The Englishman, traitor to his God and his King'; a spectre which was to rise again during the nineteenth century as 'la perfide Albion'.

Generally speaking the English, according to Boswell, thought themselves a superior race, in comparison not merely with the French, but with every other nation too. When Pastor Moritz walked through the town of Burton the locals pointed at him and hissed. In London when his maid spoke of him to the landlady she generally referred to him as 'the gentleman'; but when she was displeased with him he became 'the German'. The songs most favoured by the lower orders rang with defensive patriotism. During the Drury Lane riots in 1763, when the theatre management was attempting to do away with the institution of reduced prices for those who came in after the third act, the public clamoured for the musicians to play 'Britons, strike home', and 'The Roast Beef of Old England'. All through the reign the image of John Bull persisted, represented in various guises, sometimes in the form of the King himself, as rival to Bonaparte. But over it the typical thickset Englishman remained, full of good roast beef, open in his speech and manner, opposed to the starveling, emaciated, servile and frivolous Frenchman.

THE LANGUAGE

When George III came to the throne the language was still rich in vitality and vocabulary, but as the century declined it grew, especially in middle-class circles, more stereotyped. Jane Austen made so much use of the adjective 'nice' that it lost its real sense and no longer meant anything at all. And yet the language was still very much alive. Samuel Foote described Thomas Alexander Erskine, sixth Earl of Kellie, well-known composer and manifest bon-vivant, as having a face 'to ripen cucumbers'.

When Boswell was seeking employment with the Duke of Northumberland the Duchess wrote the polite letter of refusal customary on these occasions. ('Should anything happen in our power we should be very happy to show our inclination to serve you.') He showed it to Lord Eglinton, who referred to it as 'just three blue beans in a blue bladder'.

Pastor Moritz felt that everyday English was 'laconic but full of meaning': the populace referred to soldiers on Guard as 'lobsters' and to the bodyguard as 'fly-slicers' (for their discreet efforts to chase away with the points of their swords the flies that attacked them in the summer).

Here is a sample of dialogue relating to Mordaunt—a young blood; he had just taken his gig to be repaired, and, on deciding the account rendered for its repair to be in his view, too high, he went in search of the owner of the shop who had done the job. His

195

complaints were treated with the greatest politeness and firmness: 'Indeed, my lord, you do me injustice. I am incapable of such conduct as you tax me with, my lord.' Her tact and urbanity deserted her only when Mordaunt named her 'damned cheating old bitch'. She then placed her arms akimbo, and almost touching his face, she shouted like a virago: 'Bitch! Bitch, indeed! Not half so much of a bitch as your mother. You a lord indeed. A pretty lord . . . it must be a bit of a bastard business. . . . Bitch, truly, the mother of an honest family to be called bitch by a dirty, sneaking, pitiful lord.' Powerful language which persuaded Mordaunt to pay up, after which he climbed into his carriage and drove away to the sounds of boos and mocking laughter from the crowd which had collected meanwhile.

This strong language was soon proscribed in middle class circles. After 1791 one no longer used the word 'bitch' even in its proper sense. The female of 'dog' was now 'she-dog'. No longer were men's breeches anything but 'small clothes', which later became 'inexpressibles'. It might be that the maid was 'with child', but nothing so vulgar could happen to her mistress—she was simply 'pregnant'. In 1791 in Burton words like 'hilarity', 'stipulate', 'contemporary' and 'phenomenon' were detected in female conversation. Twenty years earlier, according to Anna Seward the poet, not only would women never have used such words, but they would not even have understood their meaning had they heard them.

THE SEARCH FOR INDIVIDUALITY

Not only was the vocabulary becoming more bland and abstract —the whole of life was becoming more orderly. There were still plenty of public holidays: the feast of the Epiphany was a very merry affair when most London shops sold 'Epiphany cakes' for a penny. At the gates of London, at Staines, agricultural workers with flowers in their hats came looking for work; and articles sold at this fair—most household objects—were laid out on brightly painted carts. In Norwich Parson Woodforde never failed to attend the big procession in honour of Bishop Blaise, the patron of wool-combers and curer of throat diseases. In every village a race was held in which women competed in their shifts or smocks—the 'shift-race'.

But gradually these aspects of everyday life began to disappear.

Transport was developing, along with the organization of industry, progress in education, and a stricter way of life, all of which tended to stamp out the individuality of people as well as of things. One man born in the year of George III's coronation wrote that everywhere one saw the same money-grubbing and mean spirit, an intolerable monotony in everything, and an irreligion which, 'spitting' in the face of Nature, was tending to change human beings into 'automats and machines'. The man who wrote in this vein was the famous eccentric, the son of the Lord Mayor, William Beckford. But as the reign declined, paradoxically enough, eccentricity itself was in no way unusual.

Eccentrics at this time were so widespread that it is difficult to pick out the really outstanding examples. But these must surely have been the 'hermits' whose one idea it was to opt out of contemporary life in some extravagant way. Beckford was one of the more extreme—he had built round his estate a wall seven miles long, to which the hares would hop up and eat out of the hands of the visitors who had come to see the Gothic tower that Beckford had erected to emphasize his proud isolation. But the hermit of Fonthill was only the most celebrated of these, he was neither unique nor the first: in 1800 when Fonthill 'Abbey' was being built, Lord Rokeby lay dying in his home, Mount Morris in Kent; there he had lived, leaving his beard and hair uncut, taking interminable baths in his innumerable out-of-door bathing-pools, refusing to attend Church—partly because of the exalted view he had of the 'Nature of the Deity' and partly because of the scant respect that he had for His ministers. In 1808 J. P. Malcolm, in his work on London, devoted several chapters to various cases of eccentricity and in 1813 a publication entitled *The Eccentric Mirror* collected together in four volumes 'Every Instance of Singularity Manifested in the Lives and Conduct of Characters who have rendered themselves eminently conspicuous by their Eccentricities'. And later a contemporary work, *The Pantheon of Eccentrics*, appeared, giving first place to perhaps the most incredible of all the eccentrics—John Mytton the squire.

John Mytton by 1810 was still a young man, but already well-known. Expelled from Harrow and Westminster schools, where in a single year he had squandered £800 and had worn out his tutor, he had put himself down for both Oxford and Cambridge without showing the least intention of attending either university, apart from arranging for three pipes of port to be sent to Cambridge. It was a fitting start to one of the finest of eccentric careers which history has ever known, but one which unfortunately comes too far outside our present study to be described in detail. Lastly there is Major Peter Labeliere, who died in 1800 (the same year as Rokeby) after expressing in his will his wish to be buried head downwards. Considering, he said, that the world he had known was upside down, he had hopes of finding himself eventually the right way up.

Towards the end of the reign eccentricity flourished as a protest against the increasing uniformity and austerity of life. It was a sign, if not of the end of the world as many believed, at least of a change so radical that, as one contemporary writer in 1815 remarked: 'The lapse of two centuries could scarcely have produced a greater alteration in these particulars [dress, etiquette and form] than could have been made by about forty years.'

INDEX

Adam brothers, 25, 28, 193
Adam, Robert, 24, 26, 28–9, 57, 59, 104
Afzelius, Adam, 62
Age of Reason (T. Paine), 55
Agriculture
  developments of, 45–6
  improvements in, 193
  progress in, 38–41
Albemarle, Earl of, 40
Alexander (water-colourist), 193
All Hallows, 79
Alliance of Church and State, The (Bishop Warburton), 143
American Revolution, 12
American War of Independence *see* War of Independence
Andreani, Count of Milan, 52
Anne, Queen, 11
  style of furniture, 26
Annual Register, The, 164
Apprentice
  life of an, 111–12
  relations between employer and, 112
Archaeological Society, 188
Archenholz, 92
Architecture
  change of, 23–6
  in churches, 149–50
Argyll, Duke of, 32
Arkwright, 51, 54
Arnold, Dr, 186
Arthur Annesley, Viscount Valentia, 131
A Serious Call to a Devout and Holy Life (W. Law), 150
Ashby, Castle, 33
Augustus Henry, Duke of Grafton, 130
Austen, Jane, 31, 195

Banks, Sir Joseph, 60
Baptists, 155

Barrington, Margaret, 190
Baskerville, 60
Bawdy houses, 135–8
Beckford, William, 32, 139, 149, 150, 176, 185, 197
Beckwith, 28
Bedford, Duke of, 102
Beevor, Reverend, 148
Bell Savage Inn, 192
Bennet, Mrs, 118
Betting and Gaming, 177–9
Big Ben (boxer), 111
Birmingham, 63
  building of canals in, 56
  industrialization of, 56–7
  riots, 55, 60–1
Blackfriars Bridge, 81
Blaise, Bishop, 196
Blenheim, 21, 32
Bonaparte, 195
Bon Ton Magazine, 139
Book of Domestic Lamentations (W. Jones), 144
Bossy, 179
Boswell, James, 58, 62, 65, 122–5, 127, 135, 136, 137, 145, 154, 175, 176, 178, 179, 182, 184, 185, 187, 189, 190, 194, 195
Boulton, John, 56
Boulton, Matthew, 51, 52, 54, 55, 56, 57–8, 59, 60, 61, 62, 63, 64, 65
Boulton, Matthew (son), 57
Bramble, Dr, 190
Brasbridge (goldsmith), 111
British Museum, 95, 191
Broadlands, 33
Brompton, 95
Bromwich, Castle, 56
Brookes, Kitty, 136
Broseley works, 54
'Brotherhood of the Friars of St Francis', 167–9
Broughton, Sir Thomas, 25
Brown, Lancelot ('Capability'), 24, 31–3

Riots
  Birmingham, 55, 60–1
  Drury Lane, 195
Roach, Mrs, 118
Rochefoucauld, François, 37–8, 40, 41
Rockingham, Marquis of, 23, 39, 177
Roderick Random, 193
Rodney, 13
Roebuck, John, 52
Rogers, farmer, 144
Rokeby, Lord, 197, 198
Romaine, William, 161
Rose, 51
Roubiliac, 194
Rousseau, 182
Rowlandson, Thomas, 46, 185, 186, 187
Royal Hospital, Chelsea, 192

Saint-Fond, Faujas de, 36–7, 38, 52–3, 156, 157
St George's Fields, 94
St George's Lodge, 166
St James Chronicle, 166
St James Palace, 80, 94, 97
St James Park, 94, 97, 105, 123, 126, 136
St John the Evangelist, feast of, 166
St Luke's Hospital, 79
Sandford and Merton (T. Day), 60
Sandwich, Earl of, 129, 167
Satinwood for furniture, 29
Saxe-Gotha, metal from, 62
Scarsdale, Lord, 22, 24
Scott, John, 177
Seaforth, Lord, 129
Seaton Delaval, 21
Seddon, Norman, 28
Sentimental Journey (L. Sterne), 182
Sermons (Tillotson), 150
Seven Years' War, 11–12
Seward, Anna, 196
Sex education, 125–7
Shearer, Thomas, 27, 30
Shelburne, 15
Sheraton, 26, 27, 28
Shipton, Reverend, 148
Shopkeepers in England, 66–7
Shuter, Ned, 138
Smith, Nancy, 68
Smith, Nanny, 135
Smith, Sydney, 147, 153

Smollett, Tobias, 81, 182, 190, 193
Snow Hill Factory, 57–8
Soane, Sir John, 25
Social security, introduction of, 59
Society for Constitutional Information, 15
Society for Political Information (Nottingham), 16
Society for the Defence of the Declaration of Rights (founded 1769), 14–15
'Society for the Proclamation, The', 162
'Society for the Suppression of Vice', 162, 164
'Society of Demoniacs', 168
Society of Friends of the People, 16
Southey, Robert, 114, 153, 174
Spanish war, 11–12
Spencer, Lord Robert, 131
Sports, popular, 188
Stamp duty in America, 12
Stanhope, Sir William, 168
Stanton, Elizabeth, 117
Stately homes, decline of, 21–5
State of the Poor, The (F. Morton Eden), 43
Stealing, 111–12, 116, 190
Steam engine
  importance of the, 54–5
Stendhal, 126
Stepney marsh, 95
Sterne, Lawrence, 153, 168, 182
Stock Exchange, 65, 104, 105, 107
Strudwick, James, 43–4
Strutt, 54
Stuarts, sovereign of, 11, 153
Sturges, Mrs, 132
'Sublime Society of the Beefsteaks', 167, 169
Summerson, Sir John, 103
Sunday schools, founding of, 162
Surman, Elizabeth, 117
Swediaur, Dr, 52
Syon House, 25

'Tall Dally'
  see Eliot, Grace
Tatham, Thomas, 28
Taxation, 64, 100
Taylor, Dr John, 145
Temple, Fanny, 132, 134